The Awesome Power of Questions

Dr Ian Loftus

OTHER MINDS
PUBLISHING

For more information, contact :

connect@ianploftus.com

https://ianploftus.com

Book design by Other Minds
Cover design by Other Minds

ISBN – Paper back : 9798858546955
Second Edition : September 2023

The book is dedicated to;

Susan, who only seems to ask Rhetorical questions. 'You do know it's a school night?' or, 'I wonder who left the toilet seat up?'

Dom, (16 January 1991- 04 October 2013) who now knows the ultimate answers.

Chloe. A forensic psychologist who's always looking for answers

Reuben. As a small boy he never stopped asking questions, now as a man, he's asking better ones.

Contents

Introduction - 1 -

Breaking down the Sales Process - 20 -

Where's The Pain? - 40 -

Handling Objections - 50 -

Closing and moving the sale forward - 53 -

Account management - 69 -

Other tactical sales tools - 79 -

The Summary - 97 -

End Matter-Part One - 98 -

Prospecting - 100 -

PART 2 - 124 -

Curiouser and curiouser - 124 -

Does life get in your way? - 155 -

Positive Thinking - 167 -

Critical Thinking - 179 -

End Matter-Part Two - 187 -

About the Author - 191 -

OTHER MINDS

PUBLISHING

Foreword

The first edition of *The Awesome Power of Questions* (2019) focused on questions related to the business and sales environment. But, after receiving numerous comments and suggestions from readers, I realised the importance too of asking questions to help improve our everyday lives. So, in this 2nd edition, I have expanded the content to include six additional areas where asking the right questions can be valuable, such as nurturing creativity and building personal relationships. In these sections, you will find a range of questions designed to help you navigate through these areas with confidence and improve your overall communication and understanding of the people around you. With the help of this book, you can unlock the full potential of asking the right questions in all aspects of your life.

The new areas covered in the 2nd edition are:

- Relationships
- Communication
- Self-awareness
- Creativity
- Decisions making
- Problem-solving

Asking questions can help us learn new things and expand our knowledge. By asking questions, we can seek out information and gain a deeper understanding of the world around us.

Asking the right questions also;

- Grows your knowledge and awareness;
- Helps you stay informed and relevant;
- Enables you to discover a new world of possibilities otherwise unknown to you and
- The better our questions, the better our answers

It's important to ask the right questions, but it's also vital to know what to do with the answers both in your business and your personal life.

You may read later on 'About the Author' page, as well as working fulltime in the corporate world I've also studied 'Creative Writing' as a postgrad since 2013. You won't be surprised then, I'm going to begin this book by saying that as traits go, 'Creativity' is *the* one that you should nurture both professionally and personally. If you can think creatively, it can impact on most of the areas that are outlined throughout this book. I'll cover it in more detail later but I'll give you a quick overview in the mini-Q&A below that I had with someone recently.

W h y   C r e a t i v i t y ?

- What is Creativity? For me, creativity is the ability to come up with new ideas and solutions to problems.
- What is Innovation? Innovation is when we take those creative ideas and turn them into something tangible - whether it's a product, service, or process - that adds value to the world.
- Are They Related? Definitely. Innovation depends on creativity. We can't innovate without first coming up with ideas.
- What Jobs Require Creativity? In my opinion, all jobs require creativity. Even seemingly routine jobs have opportunities for creative thinking.
- Why Do Organisations Need Creativity? Organisations benefit from creativity because it enables employees to solve problems and find new opportunities. Studies have shown that companies that encourage creativity and innovation tend to be more successful.
- Is Creativity a Strategic Priority? Yes, many organisations see creativity and innovation as primary strategic aims because they lead to profits and growth.
- Can Creativity be Trained? Yes, research shows that creativity can be improved through training and practice.
- What is the Best Way to Train People to be Creative? The best way to train people to be more creative is to identify their strengths and

weaknesses and develop a customized program that focuses on building skills.

- What Are the Biggest Barriers to Creativity at Work? The biggest barriers to creativity at work are lack of awareness of one's creative potential and a lack of understanding in organisations of how to identify, nurture, manage and develop creative thinking skills.
- How Do You Build a Culture of Creativity? To build a culture of creativity, organisations need to foster an environment that encourages experimentation, risk-taking, and open communication. It's also important to give employees the resources they need to develop their skills and pursue new ideas.

Why is creativity in business so important?

- Firstly, problem-solving: Creativity allows us to develop new and innovative solutions to problems. This is valuable in
- all areas of life, whether it be in the workplace, in relationships, or in personal growth.
- Adaptability: Creativity helps us to adapt to changing circumstances and to think outside of the box. This is particularly important in today's rapidly changing world, where new challenges and opportunities arise on a regular basis.

- Innovation: Creativity is the key to innovation, which is crucial for businesses and organisations to remain competitive and grow.
- Self-expression: Creativity allows us to express ourselves in unique and meaningful ways, which can help to foster self-confidence and a sense of identity.
- Emotional well-being: Engaging in creative activities has been shown to improve mental health and emotional well-being, reducing stress and anxiety and increasing feelings of happiness and fulfilment.

The reason why I embrace creativity 100%, (apart from being a writer) is because it allows us to approach life in a more dynamic and fulfilling way, opening up new possibilities for growth, achievement, and happiness.

Part 1

Questions for Business

Introduction

Asking good questions can make a real impact on your relationships, and it's not just about showing interest in the person you're talking to. Questions have the power to create intimacy, fulfilment, and enjoyment in relationships. They can also enhance your general communication skills and make others feel more comfortable in social situations.

But what makes questions so important and powerful? It's because they allow you to connect with others on a deeper level by reflecting genuine curiosity in them. Listening mindfully to their responses, watching their body language and being sensitive to what is left unspoken are all key components of a great conversation. By preparing yourself with interesting topics and fun questions, you can create an engaging dialogue that fosters trust and builds a relationship.

Remember, the goal is to create a balance of give and take in a relationship and in a conversation so that both parties are engaged. By being yourself and showing interest in the answers, you can create commonalities and build a long-lasting relationship. So next time you meet someone new, take advantage of the power of questions and see where it can take you.

Sales and Business Development

Selling is easy, right? Tell them what you're selling, smile, look like butter wouldn't melt in your mouth, wear a nice suit and they'll buy. Won't they? Why should you worry about asking sales questions? In fact, why are we even having this debate and why have I written a book about them?

If we're completely honest with ourselves though, it's not that simple, is it? If it was, *everyone* would be doing it. There would only ever be successful salespeople and they'd all be sat on a Caribbean beach for six months of the year, drinking Piña colada with big fat bank accounts.

I'm not on the beach writing this, because a) I don't like the heat and prefer to ski, and b) I work in the GIG economy and have a 'portfolio' of jobs mixing what I love, which is writing that doesn't pay much, and earning a crust in the real world so I can support my family and my writing. The real-world work is also quite rewarding, I give people who run small to medium sized businesses advice on running their business, especially on improving sales and business development.

I do other things too, but let's stick with the latter two for now and focus on sales. I love my job(s) because something different happens every day, especially in sales but, if you boil it down to the bare bones, I meet people I don't know and pursue them to give me money.

Collectively, how do we accomplish that? How do you get someone to buy whatever you're selling?

The short answer to my last question is, which is the premise of this book, you need to ask them and they'll tell you how. The only one that knows what they want is the client. They don't need *you* to tell them what they want.

In this book, I emphasize the importance of asking sales questions and why it's crucial to let the client do most of the talking. I will also highlight the common mistake of trying to tell the client why they should buy instead of asking them why they have previously bought or why they are interested in buying now. By doing so, salespeople can gather valuable information and align their product or service to the client's actual needs.

This book is not a shortcut to getting rich quick but a platform from which to learn an everyday skill that can boost confidence and sales, it focuses on practical and realistic techniques that can benefit salespeople in any industry.

I hate those 'Get rich Quick' books and videos by Influencers and Billionaire Gurus that strings you along to the very, very end, and the call to action is to invest $5,000 in their guaranteed money maker, or spend $999 on their exclusive online training course. I'm not trying to sell you a 'Silver Bullet' with this book, this isn't a shortcut to get rich quick, it's just an everyday skill that will definitely help boost your confidence and your sales.

In the meantime, you've bought my book. Thank you! Why did you do that? Perhaps just out of interest because you liked the cover page? Curiosity, because anything with *Power* or *Awesome* in the title floats your boat? A niggling little insecurity? Maybe you just want to fine tune your sales 'radar', or is this toe in the water just a little refresher? Am I the Holy Grail of closing the Sale? Let's dip that little pinkie for a second to try to find out.

'Ok, tell me why I should read your book?'

Crikey, how many times have we had that question at a first meeting? What would *your* response be? If you're still being honest with yourself, most salespeople would make the mistake of actually trying to tell them why they should buy. The reality is you don't know. Likewise at this stage, I don't know why you've bought my book and, at the moment, nor do you. So, don't tell them why, ask them why.

One way to answer the last question might be with something like:

"I can't tell you why you should read this book. Most of my customers buy it because it helps them close more deals. What did you think when you saw it on the shelf, with its promises of beach life and drinking even more Piña colada?"

(I absolutely know why you should read the book!!)

This simple response totally changed the direction of the conversation. By using a statement followed with a question, boom, you've turned the ball over, (I like rugby metaphors) you're on the front foot and moved from defence to attack. Well, you're not quite at the try line yet, but you've moving to a situation where you're starting to gather information to position and align your product/service to the actual needs of you client.

> *"What you tell them, they are cautious about. what they tell you, they tend to believe."*

Only the client knows what and why they are going to buy. It's your job to get them to tell you. That's why you need to learn how to ask the right sales questions.

If you're looking to improve your sales skills and boost your confidence, this book is definitely worth a read. It emphasizes the importance of asking sales questions and understanding the client's needs and desires, which can lead to more successful sales and happier clients.

As a salesperson, it's crucial to understand that the client holds the key to what and why they are going to buy. Your job is to uncover their needs and motivations by asking the right sales questions.

Without asking the right questions, you're left in the dark. You won't know what information the client needs to make a buying decision. You won't understand what's truly important to them or what factors are influencing their decision. Are they basing their decision on price, features, advantages, benefits, your relationship, or something else?

Furthermore, you won't know if others are involved in the buying process or if it's just the client. These are all critical pieces of information that you need to uncover in order to close the sale.

So, if you want to be successful in sales, you need to learn how to ask the right questions. By doing so, you can gather the information you need to position your product or service to meet the specific needs and desires of your client. Remember, the client knows best - it's up to you to get them to share their knowledge with you.

How do you solve customer problems?

Although many people believe that a good salesperson is someone who can charm their way out of any situation with their persuasive language, research indicates that the most successful salespeople are the ones who listen carefully rather than talk excessively. These salespeople know how to ask insightful and thought-provoking questions to gain a deep understanding of their prospects' needs.

Only when the salesperson truly comprehends the prospect's requirements can they offer a solution that solves their problems and results in a successful sale. Using sales questions allows you to identify the challenges and pain points that the prospect is facing.

For those who utilise a Sales Value Proposition (SVP) in their sales process, it is clear how valuable it can be in addressing these challenges. If you are unfamiliar with what an SVP is or how it works, don't worry; I have included a comprehensive section at the end of the book that will guide you through it.

Use questions to uncover why they will buy?

Have you ever encountered a customer who says,

'I'm just looking?'

Although it may seem like a brush-off, the truth is that they are actually looking for someone to help them make a decision. They need someone who can solve their problem and ease their pain.

In some cases, clients already know what they need to solve their problem and only need to find a way to obtain it. However, more often than not, clients need help to identify the right solution. This is where a skilled salesperson comes in. Clients who know what they want can easily find it on Google or call their supplier to place an order. It's when they need help that they seek the assistance of a salesperson.

'YOU NEED TO ASK SALES QUESTIONS AT EVERY POINT OF THE SALES PROCESS'.

Questions are an integral part of every stage of the sales process. You need to use sales questions to establish a connection with your prospect, get them to relax and open up during the 'getting to know each other' phase. During the needs analysis stage, open-ended sales questions help uncover their challenges, which will guide your next steps.

In the presentation or demonstration stage, you need to use alternate-choice sales questions to test close and ensure that they see value in the benefits you offer. Tie-down sales questions can also be used during the pre-close stage, as well as test closes. Finally, during the close, alternate-choice and tie-down sales questions can be used to guide them towards a final decision.

If you want to win more business, it's essential to stop telling your clients why they should buy from you and start asking them questions. The ability to use sales questions effectively is a crucial skill for anyone in business to master. By incorporating more questions into your sales process, you'll be surprised at the positive impact it can have on your forecast and pipeline.

Do you have poor sales figures?

Are you wondering why mastering the art of sales questioning is so crucial? Let me explain. Even if you already know the basics, it never hurts to refresh your understanding and discover new insights that can help you succeed in your sales career.

First of all, sales questions are not just a way to gather information from your prospects, they are a powerful tool to build trust and rapport with them. By asking the right questions, you show that you care about their needs and goals, positioning yourself as a helpful and knowledgeable advisor, not just a pushy salesperson.

Secondly, sales questions help you uncover hidden problems, objections and buying criteria that may not be immediately obvious. By asking open-ended questions and actively listening to the answers, you can dig deeper and discover the real pain points of your prospects and tailor your solutions accordingly.

Thirdly, sales questions help you differentiate yourself from your competitors. Instead of just presenting your features and benefits, you can ask questions that lead the prospect to realise why your solution is unique and superior to other options in the market.

Fourthly, sales questions help you qualify your leads and prioritize your time and resources. By asking qualifying questions, you can determine if a prospect is a good fit for your product or service and, if they have the authority, budget and timeline to make a purchase decision.

Finally, sales questions help you close more deals and maximize your revenue. By using closing and trial-closing questions, you can guide the prospect towards making a commitment, overcome objections, and confirm their satisfaction and loyalty after the sale.

So, whether you are a seasoned sales professional or a beginner, taking the time to learn and practice effective sales questioning skills can make a big difference in your results and income. Are you ready to discover the secrets of great sales questioning?

Let's jump in!

C o n t r o l

'Keep control of the sales process and keep asking questions. The prospect has to follow your lead'.

So, let's elaborate on the importance of asking the right questions throughout the sales process.
Firstly, it's crucial to understand that sales is a two-way conversation between the salesperson and the prospect. It's not just about the salesperson talking and trying to convince the prospect to buy. By asking open-ended questions, the salesperson can encourage the prospect to share their thoughts, needs, and concerns. This helps the salesperson to better understand the prospect's unique situation and tailor their pitch accordingly.

Secondly, asking questions also helps the salesperson to guide the prospect through the sales process, ensuring that they stay on track and move towards the desired outcome. This is especially important during the need analysis stage, where the salesperson can ask targeted questions to uncover the prospect's pain points and demonstrate how their product or service can solve those issues.

Lastly, asking questions can also help to overcome objections and close the sale. By addressing any concerns that the prospect may have had and providing them with the information they need to make an informed decision, the salesperson can build trust and credibility, making it more likely that the prospect will say yes.

In conclusion, keeping control of the sales process by asking questions is an essential part of successful selling. It helps the salesperson to better understand the prospect, guide them through the process, and ultimately close the sale.

Uncover areas of interest.

Let's dig a bit deeper on the importance of asking questions to gain a better understanding of the prospect's needs and how to use questions to gain agreement on important facts during the sales process.

Salespeople often make the mistake of assuming that they know why a prospect would want to buy their product or service, based on their knowledge of the features, advantages and benefits. However, it's crucial to remember that every prospect is unique and their motivations for buying may be different from what the salesperson expects.

To uncover the prospect's specific needs and motivations, the salesperson must ask targeted questions that allow the prospect to share their thoughts and concerns. By understanding what the prospect is looking for and the problems they want to solve, the salesperson can effectively position their product or service in a way that resonates with the prospect's needs.

One effective way to use questions during the sales process is to gain agreement on important facts. When presenting a solution that could provide cost reductions or improved efficiency, the salesperson can use a sales question to confirm that the prospect agrees with the proposed solution's potential benefits. This ensures that the prospect has acknowledged the fact and brings the salesperson closer to closing the sale.

> *"We think this solution will save you a minimum of 10% in labour cost, wouldn't you agree?"*

If the prospect does not agree with the assumption, the salesperson can use this as an opportunity to gain a better understanding of why and adjust their approach accordingly. The key is to gain agreement on important facts before moving towards the close.
Asking questions is crucial during the sales process to understand the prospect's unique needs and motivations. Additionally, using questions to gain agreement on important facts helps to build trust and credibility, bringing the salesperson closer to closing the sale.

Secure small wins

In the world of sales, it's important to understand that there's rarely a single 'magic' phrase or technique that will win you the sale. Instead, it's a gradual process that builds momentum over time, with each small agreement leading to the ultimate decision to purchase your product or service.

One technique that can be helpful in eliciting these minor agreements is the use of tie-down sales questions. These are questions that are designed to get the prospect to agree with you on a series of small points, gradually building momentum towards the final close.

For example, in a photocopier sales situation, you might ask a question like:

> *"You stated that having the ability to print documents over the network was important, is that right?"*

This helps to establish an area of agreement between you and the prospect and makes it easier to move the conversation forward.

Then, you could follow up with a more specific question:

> *"In the demo, we demonstrated that this machine will print all you need and*

Again, this is a tie-down question that seeks to elicit a minor agreement from the prospect, building momentum towards the final close.

Of course, tie-down questions can be tailored to fit any situation or industry. The key is to ask questions that help you obtain minor agreements throughout your sales presentation, building momentum and increasing the likelihood of a successful close. By using questions to establish areas of agreement with your prospect, you can make the sales process smoother and more effective.

I s o l a t e   o b j e c t i o n s

One of the biggest challenges that salespeople face is handling objections. A lot of salespeople fall apart when someone starts to raise objections. If you want to be at the top of the sales board every month or at the end of the year, then understand that you need objections in the sales process to make a sale. If they don't object to something, they don't care. However, objections are actually a necessary part of the sales process. If a prospect doesn't raise any objections, it could mean that they're not really interested in your product or service. Therefore, it's important to learn how to handle objections effectively in order to close more sales and be successful in your sales career.

To effectively handle objections, it's crucial to use sales questions to isolate and understand them. Most prospects will give you one reason for not making a buying decision on the first attempt. However, it's important to determine if the objection is real, an excuse, or if they simply don't understand your product or service. To do this, you can use sales questions to get to the root of the objection.

For example, let's say a prospect tells you they don't like the colour of your product. Instead of dismissing the objection, you can use a sales question to clarify and understand the issue. By repeating the objection back to them in the form of a question, such as 'You didn't like the colour?', you're asking for more information and getting to the root of the problem. This can help you to better understand the objection and make a new proposal that addresses their concerns.

It's also important to use sales questions to determine if an objection is real or just a dodge. By asking the right questions, you can uncover the true reason behind the objection and address it in a way that satisfies the prospect. This can help to build trust and credibility and, ultimately, lead to a successful sale.
In summary, objections are a necessary part of the sales process and should be embraced rather than avoided. By using sales questions to isolate and understand objections, you can address them effectively and increase your chances of closing more sales.

It's how you ask

The success of your sales process depends heavily on your ability to ask relevant and quality sales questions. If you're struggling in any areas of the sales process, take a moment to assess if you could benefit from asking more questions instead of simply telling your clients about your product. Asking the right questions at the right time and in the right manner and tone can make a significant difference in improving your close ratio and propelling you to sales superstardom.

Many salespeople seek out sales methodologies, sales models, buyer insights, or a 'silver bullet' to make closing the sale easier or quicker. However, the key to success lies in asking the right questions. This book aims to provide an interesting read that is not too 'salesy' and avoids excessive jargon and acronyms. I want to inform readers and provide them with valuable lists of questions, there's over 500, that they can use throughout the sales process.

Although there are many aspects of the sales process that I could have written about, the focus of the book is on providing a handful of the most valuable questions at the right time. Whether it's starting to build client relationships, handling objections, or discovering what keeps clients awake at night, this book covers all the questions you need to know. It even includes some closing techniques to help you seal the deal and book that sun-bed on a beach in St. Lucia.

So, if you're looking for a comprehensive list of sales

questions, this book has got you covered.

How to use this book

Treat this book like a cookbook, dip in an out as you would when you're looking for a recipe. Some of the questions will be really appropriate for your industry and what you sell, so you won't need to amend them at all. In general, I've tried to keep it general, so everyone reading the book can understand the underlying premise and the reason for a particular question in that particular situation. Other questions will need tweaking slightly and others might not be applicable.

Do you remember at school when you wanted to ask the teacher a question, but you were too frightened and thought you'd get made fun of?

> *"There's no such thing as a stupid question Ian, if you don't know, you don't know!" said Mr Prince, who taught maths, drove a battered old Ford Anglia and thought he was helping me.*

Well, I disagree! I've lost deals by asking stupid questions, or by not asking enough focused, accurate or appropriate ones. Your probes must be laser guided but not cutting, they must not hack your client off.

In sales there are such things as stupid questions, so make sure that your questions have a purpose and that you ask them in the right way.

Questioning is an art form and when you get it right, you'll be someone who comes across as an expert in your field, and who champions and cares about their product or solution. So please put the time and effort into mastering your art.

To be fair to Mr Prince, in an educational environment he was probably right, we'll come onto that when we discuss Socrates in the second half...

In every section, I've given you more questions than you'll *ever* need. So, in the longer lists, my top ten questions are at the beginning of each list.

Breaking down the Sales Process

Building rapport

Although rapport should be built all throughout the sales interaction by how you verbally interact with the prospect, your body language gestures like mirroring and through active listening skills. When you first meet with a prospect you need to break the ice quickly, and this can be when you first meet them at reception, as you walk together to their office or meeting room, on the phone and when you're on the way out of the meeting or at the end of the call too.

Remember, rapport building is not a stage of the sales process. You should be building rapport at all times and all throughout the sales process.

Unhappy bedfellows

In my view, getting to meet new people is one of the nicest parts of the sales process, apart from getting ink on paper of course! Clearly, you do meet the odd creep but, in general, most buyers want to get on and do their job. If it's a complicated sale, for example software, they know that they may need to work with you for some time.

Please do not think that building rapport just covers topics like the weather, favourite football teams or cheesy comments on how beautiful their kids look from the photos on their desk. Instead, you should build rapport by keeping things light but professional and business like.

And here's the warning! Under no circumstances do you flirt to close the sale, it can go wrong in so many ways.

What do I mean by flirt? Well, for example, leaving that extra button undone on the shirt, batting the old eyelashes or going over the top with the Lynx. It just needs a jealous employee to see you flirting with the buyer who then has a word with the economic buyer and you are toast. A worse case could even be that the buyer is very professional and sees flirting as a substitute for an inferior product. People buy from people, so sell yourself as a knowledgeable and reliable professional.

The Questions

- 'I noticed on your LinkedIn profile that you've only been here for 3 months. How are you settling in?'
- 'I noticed on your LinkedIn profile that you used to work for ABC Company. I used to work for them/we've done work for them/ what did you do there?'
- 'Looking on your website I noticed that you've just done this/achieved that/won this contract/moved to bigger offices/ (anything newsworthy to talk of) how's that going?'
- 'How's business?'
- 'How long have you been with the company?' (If you don't know via LinkedIn)
- 'So, you've been with ABC for 5 years?' (If you do know via LinkedIn)
- 'So, you're the title/position. What exactly does that entail?'
- 'So as the title/position, do you also oversee...'
- 'How many people in your department/do you manage/do you employ?'

- 'How long have you been in that/this field all together?'
- 'How long have you been in the/this business?'
- 'How did you get your start in the business/field?'
- 'How did your company/business that you own get started?'

- 'How many people do you manage?'
- 'Does your company have other locations?'
- 'Does your role involve a lot of travelling?'
- 'How do you keep up to date on important information in the industry?'
- What periodicals do you read?'
- 'What are you up to this weekend?' (On the way out of office/meeting/end of call)
- 'What have you got planned for the rest of the day?' (On the way out of office/meeting/end of call)
- 'What have you got on for the rest of the day?' (On the way out of office/meeting/end of call)

Setting the Scene

Before you get started, it is essential to be organised and set the scene for the meeting. For example, send out an agenda prior to the meet and ask if the

prospect wants to add anything that they want to cover.

Too many sales meetings meander aimlessly from the very start and invariably end in a no sale.
When you get this part right, you'll indicate that you're starting as you mean to go on, so you can condition your prospect on what to expect not only during the meeting itself but also what to expect from you moving forward as well.

If you make a strong start to the meeting then everything

you say and do from later in will be seen in a positive light. Similarly, if this first meeting doesn't go well, then you'll have an uphill battle for the rest of your interaction.

When setting the stage, you must make sure the prospect is aware of what you are going to do, approximately how long it will take, what the final steps will be (if you will ask for a decision or set up another meeting) and what the follow up steps will be. You need to outline the process and confirm that the prospect understands and agrees.

The Questions

- 'Well, thanks for seeing me today, John. What I'd like to do is really get to understand the situation you're in and understand your requirements and then I'll be able to see how
- we can help you. Does that sound okay to you?'
- 'So, as I mentioned on the telephone, today's meeting should only take about 30 minutes and what I will do is show you exactly how our software works and why it is so powerful. I will demonstrate how much time and money it can save your IT Dayepartment. Then, if everything looks good to you, we'll arrange a time for us to come back and install a trial version. How does that sound?'
- 'What we will go over today is.... does that sound acceptable?'

- 'So today, I am going to ....and then I'll be able to see which of our solutions is the best fit for you. Is that what you had in mind?'
- 'Our objective this morning is to first perform a comprehensive examination of your network procedures. As I had mentioned in our last meeting, this will take about two hours. Then we will analyse the information for a few days and get back to you with our recommendation. Is that what you were expecting?'
- 'Over the next 20 minutes or so, I'll show you exactly how we are able to help your retail sales people close more sales. Then I'll detail our pricing structure and see what you think... Okay?'
- 'I am going to ask you a series of questions to see if I can determine the problem. Is that okay?'
- 'In order to do this, I am going to have to ask you several questions and some may be a little sensitive. Is that okay with you?'
- 'In our discovery meeting, we will get into a few rather touchy areas...will that be alright?'
- 'This meeting will only last about an hour, as I mentioned. However, it is best if we are not interrupted. Can you see to that for us?'
- 'We will need to tour the plant to see if the square footage is sufficient. Will we have clearance this afternoon?'
- 'So, as I mentioned, we will only need about a half hour today, but I will need both you and your wife to be present for the entire interview. Will she be with us for that time?'

- 'So, today we will go over the entire plan and to do that we will need some accounting information as well as your head of I.T. Are they available?'
- 'Our objective for today is to run a diagnostic of the system. Of course, you will have to shut down for a few hours as I had mentioned yesterday. Is that still okay?'
- 'No, it's no problem that you were running a little late. However, we do need a full 45 minutes for me to accurately show you what we have. Do you still have that time available?'
- 'As I mentioned, during this portion of the process, I will have to actually get a look at your books. Do I have your permission to do that?'
- 'Okay, as planned, today we will test drive the system. I will need a temporary administrative-level password and security access. Do you have the authority to make that happen?'
- 'As we always do after an installation, we talk to the employees to see how they feel about the new service. May we have permission to talk to your people?'
- 'For my presentation, I will need a big screen and an HDMI connection. Can you set that up for us?

Revealing the real needs and wants

At the heart of every sale is an initial thorough fact-find and I always like to do a business diagnostic too, free of charge. This involves isolating the area in the client's business where your product fits in and do some analytics around that section and how it's generally performing (without your proposed solution).

In the fact find, you'll want to unearth the needs, the

wants and the desires of your prospect so you can present your products and solutions back, in a way that will be of benefit to them and fix their pain.
The only way that you can do this is to ask quality questions so you can really find out what their current situation is, what their requirements are and what they are looking to achieve.

Remember, your prospects want a good listening to, not a good talking to! They don't want to just sit there listening to your monologue of why your products and services are the best.
Once you boss this stage you will have a big advantage over your rivals. A prospect wants to know that you understand not only their business but their current problematic situation in detail.

Chances are that your competitors are asking questions but they'll only be skin deep. Instead, you need to drill down to the root causes of the issues that they face at a much deeper level and demonstrate your expertise on the subject.

The Questions

- 'How can we help?'
- 'Could you please give me some background to this?'
- 'Why are you wanting to do this particular (work/project/engagement)?'
- 'Why isn't this particular technology/service/product/situation/issue working for you right now?'
- 'Can you tell me more about the present situation/problem?'
- 'How long has it been an issue/problem?'
- 'How long have you been thinking about this?'
- 'How is it impacting your organisation/customers/staff?'
- 'How much is the issue/problem costing you in time/money/resources/staff/energy?'
- 'How much longer can you afford to have the problem go unresolved?'
- 'When you went to your existing suppliers and shared your frustrations about this problem, what reassurances did they give you that it wouldn't be repeated?'
- 'How did these problems/issues first come about? What were the original causes?'
- 'How severe is the problem?'

- 'Why do you think the issue/problem has been going on for so long?'
- 'When do you need the issue/problem fixed by?'
- 'What kind of return or payoff will you be looking for if you get a successful resolution of the problem?'
- 'How often do you think the problem has come up where you weren't even aware of it?'
- 'Who is ultimately responsible for this?'
- 'Tell me more about it.'
- 'Can you make an educated guess as to how much it costs you?'
- 'Why have you been dealing with this for so long?'
- 'Why do you think it is happening?'
- 'What's your role in this situation/issue/problem?'
- 'What bothers you the most about this situation/issue/problem?'
- 'What are you currently doing to address the problem?'
- 'What have you done in the past to address the problem?'
- 'Have you used this type of product/service in the past?'
- 'Does this affect other parts of the business?'
- 'What has prevented you from fixing this in the past?'
- 'What kind of timeframe are you working on to fix this?'
- 'How long have you been thinking about it?'
- 'Who else is aware of it?'
- 'What is it costing you?'
- 'What is your strategy to fix this problem?'

- 'Who supports this action?'
- 'Is this problem causing other problems?'
- 'What practical options do you have to address this?'
- 'What kind of pressure is this causing you and the business?'
- 'Does your competition have these problems?'
- 'What goals and objectives do you have in general for this?'
- 'What is your biggest challenge with this?'
- 'What has made you want to look into this now?'
- 'In a perfect world, what would you like to see happen with this?'
- 'What are your key objectives with this?'
- 'What options are you currently looking at?'
- 'What options have you tried?'
- 'What do you like about your current supplier?'
- 'What kind of time frame are you working within?'
- 'How important is this need (on a scale of 1-10)?'
- 'What is the biggest problem that you are facing with this?'
- 'What other problems are you experiencing?'
- 'What are you using/doing now?'
- 'If you could have things the way you wanted, what would it look like?'
- 'Do you have any preference with regards to the solution?'
- 'Is there anything I have overlooked?'
- 'Have I covered everything off?'
- 'What alternatives have you considered?'
- 'Have you got any questions you'd like to ask me?'

- 'What is important to you in finding a solution to this?'
- 'What are your top 3 requirements that this solution just has to have?'
- 'How soon would you like to move with this?'
- 'What 3 key outcomes do you want from this?'
- 'How does this look/sound/feel to you?'
- 'Can you please tell me about that?'
- 'Can you give me an example?'
- 'Can you be more specific?'
- 'What other factors have we not discussed that are important to you?'
- 'Are there any other areas I haven't asked you about that are important to you?'
- 'What sense of urgency do you have here?'
- 'What else should I know?'
- 'If you could design the perfect solution, what would it look like, how much would you spend and how long would it go for?'
- 'What are the long-term effects of the problem?'
- 'What are the intangible effects of the problem?'
- 'Do you know what other areas the problem is costing you money?'
- 'Can you put an amount on the problem in terms of cost: Weekly, monthly, annually?'
- 'Can you see how much money you/your organisation loses every day by not solving this issue?'
- 'Does the issue cause problems with employee moral?'
- 'Does the issue cause problems that negatively affect the motivation of your staff?'

- 'Can this problem affect productivity?'
- 'Who/how does the problem ultimately affect your current customers?'
- 'How does the problem ultimately affect your prospective customers?
- 'How does the problem ultimately affect your sales teams?
- 'How does the problem ultimately affect your other employees?
- 'How does the problem ultimately affect your sales process?
- 'How does the problem ultimately affect your pricing/selling costs?'
- 'How does the problem ultimately affect your reputation/goodwill/brand?
- 'Can you see how this problem/issue can give your competition a competitive advantage?'
- 'If you were in your competitors' shoes, how would you take advantage of this?'
- 'If you were your competition, what would you do right now?'
- 'Do you know what your competition is thinking/planning about this?'
- 'Do they suffer the same problem?'
- 'Do your competitors also have this problem or is it unique to your organisation?'
- 'Is this an industry wide problem?'
- 'Is it regional/geographical/demographical?'
- 'How much does this problem cost you in man hours/time?'
- 'How much more productive could your people be if problem did not exist?'

- 'So, what type of a number would you put on this?'
- 'Looking at this from a point of lost sales, how much is just ONE sales worth to the company?'
- 'Who did you work with last time and why?'
- 'Thanks for all of the information that you've given me, it's been really useful. Have I asked you about every detail that's important to you?' (This is a 'last chance saloon' question which enables the prospect to cover anything you may not have asked about but was important to them!)

S h o w   m e   t h e   M o n e y

At the very earliest opportunity, when qualifying a prospect, you need to ask what the budget is that they've got to work with, or indeed if they have got the budget or are they on a fishing trip. If they have got money, are they in the same ball park as your products and services?

Some prospects feel comfortable when talking about money.

Others do not, and will keep their cards close to their chest!
Some will know what the budget is and others will not. If this is the later, then you could be dealing with the wrong

person, not the decision maker. Dig deeper.

Some will know what the budget is and tell you they don't have one!

So, there are lots of games that are played when it comes to establishing budget.

T h e   Q u e s t i o n s

'We've got a number of options available; what were you looking to pay so I can match the right solution at the right price for you, just a ballpark...?' (Say 'just a ball park' very casually as though it's no big deal)

- 'Have you got a ballpark figure in mind? Just a ballpark...'
- 'What are you working with at the moment? Just a ballpark...'
- 'Have you got budget approval for this already?'
- 'How do you handle budget considerations?'
- 'How will this product/project get funded?'
- 'What sort of budget do you have in mind?'
- 'What are you looking to pay for this?'
- 'We've got a number of options available; what were you looking to pay so I can match the right solution at the right price for you?'
- 'Is there budget allocated for this project?'
- 'Whose budget will support this initiative?'
- 'Have you arrived at a budget or investment range for this project?'
- 'Are funds allocated, or must they be requested?'

- 'What is your expectation of investment required?'
- 'So we don't waste any time, are there any budget parameters to remain within?'
- 'Have you done this before and at what investment level?'
- 'What are you looking to spend on this?'
- 'Are you working within a budget for this?'
- 'Have you got a ballpark figure in mind?'
- 'Does your budget, to solve the problem, match the severity of the problem?'
- 'The last time something like this happened, how much did it cost you to fix it?'
- 'What are your time and budget goals on this?'
- 'As important as this is, I don't imagine you have a blank cheque to get it done... how much are you working to, to get this fixed?'
- 'If you had unlimited funds, I could very easily put together a package to solve all the issues. Since I know that is not the case, I'll stay within the limits you give me. So, what is your overall budget for this?'
- 'So, what is your range on this? I mean, in a perfect world, what is the minimum amount you would like to see me get this done for? Then, what is the maximum you could possibly put into this, if it became absolutely necessary?'
- 'Now, will you handle this solely from your department's budget? Or would you be working with other departments?'
- 'So, what is your department's input in terms of the overall budget?'

- 'You said the problem is costing you £X a year. So how does your budget to fix it match up with that?'
- 'From what you've told me, this issue cost your organisation £X every month?'
- 'So, what are you going to invest to stop that?'
- 'With what you told me, I can see that your organisation will spend £X over the next few months if this problem is not resolved. So, how much have you budgeted to prevent spending that money again this year?'
- 'From what you've told me, your competition is enjoying a huge advantage over you because of this. How much have you budgeted to take the lead back?'
- 'Okay, so we know this is costing you X number of sales every day/month/quarter/year. (Calculate a figure that is close to the cost of your top package). Have you budgeted at least that amount to fix this?'
- 'So, what do you think it is worth for you to get rid of this problem?'
- 'I know in the long term you will invest 10s of 1,000s however, how much are you ready to get started with?'
- 'This is a multi-faceted problem that will take time to get completely right. But for right now, how much do you have to take the first step?'
- 'How much have you budgeted for the first step in this project?'
- 'Like the old saying goes, 'You can eat an elephant if you do it one bite at a time.' How much do you want to commit for the first bite?
- 'How much can you afford right now?'

- 'What did you plan on investing in this?'

Decision Makers & Decision Making

We touched on identifying the decision maker slightly in the previous section, but I can't stress enough how vital it is that you need to know who makes the buying decisions, plus it's critical that you understand your client's decision-making process and how decisions are made, so you can manage and facilitate the whole decision-making progression.
Are you speaking to the right people? If you're not, how are you going to influence their decision making?

Who is involved in the decision process? If you don't know, how are you going to meet their requirements? It's unbelievable how much of sales people's time is wasted if they are speaking to the gatekeeper not the decision maker and they fail to understand how their client will make their final buying decision.

The only way you can get an advantage above the competition is to align the way that you sell to how they buy and you'll only discover this by asking questions. Clearly a wily buyer or decision maker, (ask the question as they could be two different people), might want to safeguard the buying process because they'll actually be telling you how to sell to them!

The Questions

- 'Is there anyone else involved in making this decision other than yourself?'
- 'Who holds the pen over this project?'
- 'Who signs the capex off in your department?'
- 'What's the process for making a decision on this?'
- 'How will you make the decision on who to select as a supplier?'
- 'How will you be evaluating the different options?'
- 'What other options are you considering?'
- 'What can you tell me about your decision-making process?'
- 'How much support does this have at senior management level?'
- 'When will you be ready to implement a solution?'
- 'When are you looking to make a decision?'
- 'How did you select your current provider?'
- 'How broad a search are you conducting for this purchase?'
- 'What's your top priority in approaching this decision?'
- 'Have you got a deadline for making this decision?'
- 'What's your key decision-making criteria when choosing a supplier?'
- 'Are you seeking formal proposals for this work?'
- 'Who will ultimately have responsibility for the successful resolution of this problem?'
- 'Who controls the resources required to make this happen?'
- 'Who has initiated this request?'

- 'Who are the main sponsors and/or champions for this?'
- 'Do you have to seek anyone else's approval to make the decision/make this happen?'
- 'After I get the proposal to you, how soon after will you decide?'
- 'How will you know who has the best solution for you?'
- 'So far, what conclusions have you reached about fixing this problem?'
- 'How do you see us helping you, and why us as opposed to someone else?'
- 'Have you decided what the best approach is to address this issue?'
- 'So how do you normally handle things like this from here? What are our next steps?'
- 'How does your organisation normally handle this?
- 'Who makes the final decision? Is that you?'
- 'Assuming that you love the proposal I put together as well as the price, what would we do after that?'
- 'Should I bring/make/prepare multiple proposals? If so, whom should I prepare them for?'
- 'Do we need anyone else to be with us when I present our solution?'
- 'Is this decision normally handled on a departmental basis, or does it have to go up the ladder?'
- 'Do you normally work with purchase orders on things like this?'
- 'Do you usually use an open P.O. for orders like this?'

- 'Assuming that you love what I bring back to you, including the price, who else has to fall in love with the offer for us to make it a reality?'
- 'Will you be working with other departments/heads/divisions on this?'
- 'So, who will pull the trigger on this?'
- 'So does the buck stop and start with you?'
- 'Assuming that I am able to deliver exactly what you want and need, are you in a position to ok the agreement today?'
- 'So, whose signature will I ultimately need to get?'
- 'Is there anyone else you have to get the approval of to get started on this?'
- 'Are you the final decision maker on this?'

Where's The Pain?

The information that you gather at this point is the corner stone of your sales plan. During all your customer interactions you need to establish the issues and problems that the prospect is facing and, vitally, the potential upside to them of implementing the solution.

The objectives of these questions are to build the pain so that they are moved to action and also to build up a picture of the benefits that they will experience by selecting your products and services.
This is a key stage of the sales process because if the prospect does not deem that the issues are serious enough then they will not be compelled to act.

Be careful when building the pain. If you're talking to an educated and sales-savvy buyer then they will see straight through what you're trying to do if you go over-board on building the pain points.

So, weigh up all of the options and build the right amount of pain and the future benefits for them to alleviate it.

T h e   Q u e s t i o n s

- 'What problem is the current situation causing you?'
- 'If you don't solve (insert the challenge here), what kind of problems will you face going forward?'
- 'If you could get this under control/sorted, what would it mean to your business?'
- 'How would implementing these changes affect your competitiveness in the market?'
- 'How would implementing these changes affect XYZ?'
- 'How will you evaluate the success of this project/implementation/product?'
- 'You mentioned that you're having issues with your current provider, if you work with us, what are you hoping will be different?'
- 'What would solving this issue/problem mean to you personally?'
- 'If you were to wave your magic wand how would this look now?'
- 'If we were able to solve your problem, what would this mean to your company?'

- 'What's the pay off with this? How much will this make you/save you in the future?'
- 'How severely has your company/department/customers/staff been affected by these problems?'
- 'What is the ideal outcome you'd like to experience?'
- 'What results are you trying to accomplish?'
- 'What better product/service/customer/staff condition are you seeking?'
- 'How will the operation/company/customer experience be different as a result of this?'
- 'What would be the return on investment with this?'
- 'How will your productivity/customer service/staff attrition/etc. be improved because of this?'
- 'What issues and problems would this alleviate?'
- 'How would your value proposition be improved because of this?'
- 'How much will you save when we implement this?'
- 'What will these results mean for your company?'
- 'How will these results impact the bottom line?'
- 'What will happen if you do nothing?'
- 'What is the scope of the impact (on customers, employees, suppliers)?'
- 'Is this a priority right now?'
- 'What outcome/result are you looking for?'
- 'Have you exhausted all options in trying to fix this yourself?'
- 'What could you have done to avoid this?'
- 'Have you made the decision that you MUST do something to address this issue?'

- 'Is there a sense of urgency to fix it or do you have plenty of breathing room?'
- 'How, specifically, will the operation/company be different when we're done?'
- 'What is the rate of return (on sales, investment, etc.) that you seek?'
- 'What performance indicators will increase or decrease if we are successful?'
- 'How will you measure success?'
- 'What kind of payoff will you be looking for?'
- 'What's the value of this problem over time?'
- 'If you did nothing, what would happen?'
- 'Let's imagine the problem is fixed, what would it look like and how would you know?'
- 'What is the date by which you hope to get the results in place?'
- 'Can you see how this issue is costing you money/sales/time/customers?'
- 'So doing XYZ the way you have been, actually costs your organisation X number of hours every day. That means you are losing £X every day/week/month/ year. Are you comfortable with that?'
- 'Did you realise that you were losing that much money/time/productivity before?'
- 'If you add up the total in annual terms, how much does this cost you?'
- 'How do you/your employees do XYZ now?' (Without your solution. Your objective here is to help the prospect see the deficits they suffer by not having your solution. Once you are able to uncover a problem or problems, they suffer by not owning

your solution, you can then attach a monetary figure, a cost to that problem.)

- 'Have you ever thought of exactly how much money/time it cost you/your organisation/your employees to do this... this way?' (Without your solution)
- 'So, what do your people do when this situation comes up today?' (Without your solution)
- 'How much do you spend on XYZ today?' (Without your solution)
- 'You are spending £X every month. (Without your solution) Have you budgeted for this loss?'
- 'Is losing this amount of money normal?'

Key Performance Indicators (KPI'S)

Sometimes this stage of the sales process is often overlooked and it's certainly an area that is brought up more often by the prospect than by the sales person. Therefore, you can really demonstrate your expertise by being proactive by working with your prospect to discuss what key performance indicators you can put in place to ensure that the product or service is a success.

> *'If you can't manage it, you can't measure it.'*
> *– My Dad (199?)*

The minimum success criteria should take the following shape, with multiple stages throughout the implementation

of the solution, whether you're a car salesman, software
seller, or an estate agent selling off plan;

- How will you know if your product or service has
  had the desired effect?
- How will you measure success?
- How will you work together with the prospect to
  ensure everything runs smoothly?

Once you've sold the solution you are now in a
'partnership' so, whether you like it or not, you're in this
deal together. Consequently, you need to agree the KPI's
together because you both need to be on the same page
when it comes to managing expectations, both in your
organisation and in your clients.

The Questions

- 'What KPI's shall we put in place to ensure this is a
  success?'
- 'How will you know we've accomplished your
  goals?'
- How will you measure this?'
- 'What indicators will you use to assess our
  progress?'
- 'Who or what will report on our results?'
- 'What are the standards that we will have to meet?'
- 'What are the immediate benchmarks we need to
  reach with the service?'
- 'What are long-term benchmarks that we should
  aim for?'

- 'Do you have a list of objectives the software will have to meet before you may take a look at an enterprise–wide system?'
- 'What departments will be involved in establishing KPI's for the new installation?'
- 'Who are involved in assessing the KPI's of our service?'
- 'Have you established key benchmarks to measure our performance?'
- 'What KPI's do you have in place to evaluate our performance over the next year?'
- 'I really appreciate your confidence, yet how will you share/report/demonstrate/prove to your boss/supervisor/superiors that we are performing as promised?'
- 'Have you established clear parameters to let us know that we are on target?'
- 'How will we know if we are on target?'
- 'How can we demonstrate that the system is operating up to par?'
- 'What do you consider par performance?'
- 'What numbers will we need to hit to be considered above par?'
- 'Do you have a solid set of goals for us to reach?'

Potential issues and barriers

On the up-side, the deal you're working on may be with an existing client that you have a great relationship with, or it might even be a very positive prospect that contacted you because a colleague referred you, happy days, easy sailing, right? No!! No matter how much the prospect may want your product or service, there might be circumstances, events or even people that could get in the way of the purchase. For example, is the prospect you're dealing with the economic buyer or just the project manager?

As a sales person you need to get these issues out in the open so you can deal with them quickly and effectively, they might include; internal politics, legacy systems, staff buy-in or even staff or management attitudes towards change, all these things can all get in the way of a purchasing decision.

If you don't tease these issues out at the start or they don't surface at all, then you may find that the prospect will hide behind a timing or price objection when really, it's something completely different. Their answers will tell you all of the indirect reasons why they may not go ahead so make sure you understand them.

The Questions

- 'What obstacles do you see that would prevent this project from going forward?'
- 'Is there anything we haven't discussed which could get in the way?'
- 'In the past, what has occurred to derail potential projects like this?'
- 'What do you estimate the probability is of this going ahead?'
- 'Have I covered everything you need to know? What, if anything, do you additionally need to hear from me?'
- 'Is there anything happening in the company at the moment that might jeopardise this?'
- 'What are your thoughts so far?'
- 'Do you have any concerns at this stage?'
- 'What are the restrictions on this project, from your side?'
- 'Does what I've said sound like what you have in mind?'
- 'Are there any issues that must be addressed first in order to seriously consider fixing this problem?'
- 'Are there any internal political issues that must be addressed before you decide to change?'
- 'What's your organisation's attitude toward change?'
- 'Are there any competing projects that could take priority over this?'
- 'What has to be in place for this deal to go down smoothly?'

- 'Assuming you make a change, what concerns would you have about the implementation step?'
- 'For all the good you are trying to achieve, do you see any unavoidable negative consequences?'
- 'Are there any issues concerning your current supplier/situation/vendor that I need to know about that may derail us moving forward?'
- 'Are there any personal issues with the current vendor/supplier that may cause us a problem? Relatives, long time friendships, etc?'
- 'Are there any future plans that may affect the project such as mergers, acquisitions, public offerings, etc?'
- 'How long have you been working with that vendor?'
- 'Do they still treat you that way they did when you were a new account?'
- 'Much of what our software does is help you save time. However, many people actually make a living off wasting time. Is there anyone who may be afraid of the software upgrade?'
- 'This upgrade is going to eliminate a lot of overtime hours for a lot of people. Do you think that may cause a problem?'
- 'Our installed software is so efficient; it could possibly eliminate a job position or two. Is that going to be a problem?'
- 'Some people see technological advances as a threat. Do you have anyone like that in your department?'

Handling Objections

Most salespeople HATE objections, they think they're going backwards in the sale or even losing the sale if the prospect says 'No.' In reality, objections are not a bad thing, all they mean is that you haven't built up sufficient value to your proposition, you've not relieved their pain, or they don't see your products and services as a MUST compared to what they have to pay.

There are two ways to increase the perceived value in your solution. You can either increase the severity of the prospects pain or you can increase the value of the solution. By asking some well-crafted questions you can get to the real issues, correct the perception quickly and effectively and happily get the sale back on track.

In resolving your prospects objections, the ability to ask some probing questions and in the right tone is very important.
You might need to clarify some aspects of what you've said if the client isn't clear and at the same time establish exactly what the prospect means.

The Questions

- 'Exactly what do you mean by that?'
- 'Exactly what do you mean by too expensive?' (Compared to what?)

- 'I understand, but let me ask you a quick question. Do you like the idea/proposal/product? I mean, does it make sense?' (Try to gauge interest by their response)
- 'Can you see how it will save/improve/better your money/time/resources both today and into the future?' (Gauge if you did a solid sales interaction and the prospect can see and believe in the benefits)
- 'Who do you think will lose the most if you do not take action?' (Express the reality)
- 'Why do you feel that way?'
- 'If we resolve this, can we then move forward?' (Isolating the objection)
- 'What were you looking to pay?'
- 'What would satisfy you?' (Make the buyer answer the objection.)
- 'What can we do to overcome that?' (Makes the buyer answer the objection and demonstrates joint accountability).
- 'When do you think is best to solve a problem like this?'
- 'When you say too expensive/cost too much/etc., are you referring to the price or the cost?'
- 'Are you saying you can't afford to continue paying the cost of the problem or you can't afford the solution?'
- 'I completely understand that you want to think about it, but please allow me to help you with that... what is it that you want to think about? I'll be thinking about it too, and that way we can come up with an answer faster.'

- 'Of course, I understand that you want to think about it. Please help me so that I know that I didn't leave out any important information. What is it that you need to think about? (Do not wait for an answer to this question, instead begin immediately posing possible answers)
- 'Is it the guarantees we offer that you need to think about?'

(Pose questions that present the benefits of your solution. For every answer the prospect says is not the thing they need to think about; they help you narrow down the options to get to the real objection and help the prospect see that there is no objection or leave you with an objection you can turn into a positive buying decision.)

- 'I apologise. If you need to think about it, then I must not have given you all of the information you need to decide. Let me double check... Did I show you how this solution will solve the problem today and in the future?'
- 'Was I able to show you how our solution pays for itself?'
- 'Did I show you how our solution is custom tailored to your office?' (As before, ask questions that express each benefit).
- 'Did you like what I showed you?'
- 'Was I able to show you that over the next few months you will actually pay the cost of our solution if you don't buy it?'

- 'Can you see that the benefits of the solution will not only save you time/money today, but well into the future?'
- 'I appreciate your concern. Can I tell you how we handled this issue when I worked with ABC Company?

Closing and moving the sale forward

So, you've answered all the objections, you've created value and matched your solution to the prospect's requirements and, if you've done a good job managing the sales process then closing should be the logical next step. There's no real need for gimmicky closing lines or so-called tricks that sales people in the 80's and 90's used to come out with, you're a professional. However, you still need to ask for the business in some way.

At the end of a meeting a 'close' might not even be to ask for the order, you might be closing for the next meeting or to get in front of the real decision maker, or even just to get onto the tender list.

Depending on what you need to 'close on' will determine which line of questioning you'll need to use. This is another area that sales people generally struggle with, simply just 'asking for the order', so I thought it was worth taking a few minutes of your time and dedicate them to this section.

I read a paper just recently that really dismissed this kind of salesmanship, saying it was old hat etcetera. Strangely enough, it used exactly these principles within, to try and sell their new thinking!!

There are a number of ways to close so I've highlighted and explained the main ones over the following few pages.

Assumptive close - Technique

Act as if the other person has made the decision already. Turn the focus of the conversation towards the next level of questions, such as how many they want, when they want it delivered, what size they need, and so on.

- 'When shall we deliver it to you?'
- 'What will your friends say when they see it?'
- 'Will 20 cases be enough?'
- 'Where will you put it?'

How it works

The Assumptive Close works by the Assumption principle, where acting confidently as if something is true, makes it difficult for the other person to deny this. For them to say you are wrong would be to cast themselves as an anti-social naysayer.

The assumptive close does however help put sales professionals in a better state of mind because they assume that the customer is going to make a purchase. As long as the sales person makes sure that each step of the sales process is covered and provides enough value to the customer, assuming a sale will close is a powerful and highly effective closing technique. If you learn only one close, this is the one to learn.

The key thing about the assumptive close is that you need to take frequent 'temperature checks' of your customer to make sure that she is following along with your assumption-of-sale. There's nothing to specifically say to enact this technique except to be as uber confident as possible in your product and yourself.

Assumption principle

If you act as if something was true, I may well believe you. Some of us might call that a 'bluff', however, I strongly recommend you to only tell the truth about your service and product to your clients.

How it works

If I act as if something is true, then other people around me have two choices. They can either assume I am lying or they can assume I am telling the truth.

Generally, as professional sales people or buyers, we assume people are telling us the truth unless we have already decided that we distrust them. Underlying this and you might ague it's a sweeping principle, psychologically as humans we believe that most people are trustworthy, consequently a decision that the other person is lying would cause conflict and no one likes disagreement, so we assume they are telling the truth.

This is the principle of the Emperor's New Clothes. Two crooks convince the emperor that they weave the finest cloth in the land and he pays a huge amount of money and orders some new clothes. He sends two representatives to see the clothes being made, but there's no cloth only empty looms and needles without thread. The men not wanting their boss to think they're stupid, tells him his new outfits are well worth the investment. Even when the emperor puts on the non-existent clothes he too goes along with the assumption. Eventually he goes out on a royal parade and his subjects line the streets, they too buy into the emperor's new clothes also not wanting to look stupid or disagree. It's only when a small child points out that the emperor is actually naked, that the truth comes out.

Assumption is a part of creating a self-fulfilling prophecy, where your belief in something leads to it coming true. Not magically, but through the conscious and subconscious actions in which you consequently engage. This is the principle used in change management where an effective leader has a vision and then lives and breathes it until it comes true.

How to use it

Like the Emperor who desperately wanted the finest clothes money could buy, act 'as if' what you want was true. If the other person challenges it or acts confused, be concerned for them. The 'assumptive close' of selling assumes the other person already wants to buy, so you say something like

'DO YOU WANT THE BLUE ONE OR THE RED ONE?

Alternative close

The alternative close is similar and works by offering more than one clearly defined alternative to the customer. The number of alternatives should be very few - two or three is often quite adequate. If you offer too many alternatives, the customer will then be faced with a more complex problem of how they choose between the many alternatives offered.
Note that this technique works well in many different situations where you are seeking agreement, and not just selling products.

An extra technique that can be effective is to add a slight nod when offering the preferred choice. This can be accompanied by subtle verbal emphasis on the words.

Examples:

- 'Shall we meet next Monday or is Wednesday better for you?'
- 'Would you prefer the red one or the blue one?'
- 'Would you like one packet or two?'
- 'Which of these three widgets seems the best fit for you?'

How it works

The Alternative Close is a variant on the broader-based Assumptive Close and works primarily through the assumption principle, where you act as if the customer has already decided to buy, and the only question left is which of a limited number of options they should choose.

Other closing techniques

The Assumptive or Alternative Close often happens without thinking and we use them instinctively, but no matter how hard you work during the sales process, handling objections providing the right solution that meets the customer's needs if you can't ask for the order or are weak in closing the sale, all that hard work is wasted and you will suffer in your career. While closing comes naturally to some people, others will hopefully benefit from studying and practicing the following tried and tested techniques to help overcome any fear.

Learning how to close is just like when you learned about

the features, advantages and benefits of your product or service, it takes time and patience. Learning how to close will also take time, patience, and lots of practice, even if that's in front of the mirror or when you're driving along in your car. I often pretend I'm on the phone to someone instead of talking to myself in the car.

The takeaway close

Don't you just hate it when things are taken away from you, whether it is something we own or something that we want to own. That feeling when you see something advertised, go to the shop and they've sold out, or haven't got your size.

The takeaway close is similar, it involves reviewing certain features or benefits a customer has said is important and then suggesting that they forgo some of these features — perhaps to offer cost savings. Bam, this has a psychological impact on customers because they don't want to lose anything on their wish list and it just might influence them to buy now.

A variation of this is the Time limited Offer (TLO) close which puts a time frame on a special deal, then it's taken away and the standard deal is put back on the table. Another variation of the TLO is the next closing technique.

The Columbo close

Not only was the TV character Columbo a fantastic police detective, but he was also an exemplary sales coach. While few think of Columbo as a sales professional, his famous one-liner has led to more sales than almost any other line in sales history.

The classic Columbo close was the line he often used after the suspects thought Columbo was done speaking to them. He would turn and start to walk away and just when the suspect began to breathe a sigh of relief, Columbo would turn and say,

'JUST ONE MORE THING…'

After you've wrapped up your sales pitch and you know the customer is about to walk away, use the Columbo line to hit the customer with the most enticing part of your pitch. It works whether you're selling cars, life insurance or timeshare.

The puppy dog close

Who can resist a cute puppy? Take a dog lover into a pet shop and he'll go gaga. Offer to let the dog lover take a puppy home to 'try it out' and nine out of 10 times the customer will buy the puppy. For sales professionals who have the option of allowing their prospects to 'test drive' or 'try' their product, the puppy dog close has a very high closure rate.

If you've ever purchased a car, the sales professional more than likely used the puppy dog close on you. Using a puppy dog close is a low-pressure and highly effective method to get a customer to sign on the bottom line. Once you're aware of the technique, you'll see your sales numbers steadily improve.

The backwards close

Most sales professionals were taught that sales cycles followed a predetermined number of steps, with step one being the 'prospecting and qualifying' step. But what if you started with the final step, asking for referrals? It is the backwards closing technique that starts where most sales end.

What most backward closing technique users experience is that they feel that the customer is immediately put at ease when they realise that you are not trying to sell them something. After that, it's smooth sailing to explain the product and its benefits and value — and then sign the deal.

The now or never close

If you want to push a customer to make a purchase right away, try offering them a one off some special benefit. You might say:

*'We only have one item left at this price,
and it'll be going up next week.'*

*'If you sign up by the end of the day
today, i can give you 10 % off.'*

This approach is effective because people are often afraid
to make a decision and commit — even if they
want the product. This way, you cut through their inertia.
You already demonstrated that the product has value and
meets their needs and you're not offering them money
because the product is defective or being phased out.

T h e   s u m m a r y   c l o s e

When you summarise the benefits and value of the
product you're offering, it's easier for a prospect to sign on
the dotted line. That's because it can be difficult for some
people to differentiate between two or three different
products.

For example:

*'So, we have the compact Startrucks
espresso machine that has a tiny counter
space footprint. it comes with a built-in
chocolate sprinkler, and it has a 2-year
warranty. we also offer free delivery.'*

If you help the prospect mentally visualise what they're

purchasing — and sum it up in a concise way — it's easy for them to understand they're actually getting what they want.

The hard close

Hard closing normally comes in when you've tried everything else and should only be used when you have nothing to lose. While people generally love to buy things, most hate being 'obviously' sold to. When it comes to the hard close, customers are well aware that you are selling them something. And to be fair demands a lot of courage and confidence and not for the faint hearted.

This is eyeball to eyeball, first to blink, show no fear, get-the-deal-signed type of selling. Despite its negative reputation, sometimes the hard close is the best closing technique to use. The one caveat is that you should never use it too early in the sales cycle.

I'll stress my point on this one because, like it or not, sometimes the only sales closing technique that will work is a hard close. Often associated (and often incorrectly) with used car sales professionals, hard closing is not usually fun or enjoyable. While being able to hard close may earn you respect from your fellow sales professionals, it won't help you build long-lasting customer relationships. Hard closing is not for everyone and should only be used when either you have no other closing skills or nothing else is working.

When to use the Hard Close

There are some customers that, no matter how much value you have built into your product or service, or how amazing your presentation was, you will not or cannot get a buying decision.

Though it may seem brutal, it may be time for you to pull out the hard close from your bag of sales tools.

The reason that the hard close should only be used when all else fails is that using the hard close is either all or nothing. With most other types of closes, if the customer says 'no,' you still have the possibility to try to close the sale again at a later date.

But when you employ the hard close and the customer says no, chances are there's no going back and you have to walk away, losing the deal and the customer.

Things to consider when deciding if you should use the hard close, but to repeat myself only use this big boy when you've exhausted every option and have nothing else to lose.

Are you ready?

If you have determined that you have nothing to lose and have preferably consulted with either your sales manager or a colleague you respect, it's time to get into the hard-close state of mind. Even before you meet the prospect you need to decide that you will not stop closing until you are either asked to leave, your prospect becomes visibly angry, or you hear at least five 'Nos''.

Do some pre-call planning to map out your approach. Relying on your quick wit and ability to 'spin' is often not enough to successfully complete a hard close. Write down all the possible customer objections that you can think of and how you will respond to these objections. Each of your objection responses must end with a closing question. Whether that closing question is simply 'can we move forward now?' or 'does that make sense to you?' doesn't really matter. What does matter is that you satisfy the customer's objections, one by one, and move on to either the next objection or to the final closing question?

Most rookie sales people and, to be honest unsuccessful ones, stop closing after the first 'no' they hear from their customers. The fact is that most sales require getting past three 'no' responses, and several take a few more. Though there is no golden rule, stopping your closing attempts after five refusals is a good rule of thumb. Any more and you risk not only getting the customer very angry but also having them harm your reputation in their networking circles.

Is the prospect ready?

Hard closes create stress, fear, anger, resentment, and lots of other unpleasant emotions for customers. They know you are trying to close them and that they either don't want to buy from you or have not been convinced to do so yet. When you begin your close, their walls will immediately go up. Depending on how well they manage their stress, they will either become sharper or duller with their thoughts.

If they become smarter, you need to be even sharper and more realistic that you probably won't be able to get the deal closed. If, however, their ability to think on their feet becomes weaker, you need to respond quickly and use trial closes as often as you can.

The key point to remember is that during a hard close, the person with the most confidence and certainty will win.

The Questions

- 'How would you like to move ahead?'
- 'When would you like to move ahead?'
- 'Shall I book some time in to kick this off?'
- 'Shall I make the arrangements to get this ordered?'
- 'Is it better to get this started immediately, or wait for XYZ to happen?'
- 'Is there anything at all from preventing us moving forward?'

- 'I can schedule two days next week to make a start?'
- 'Can we proceed?'
- 'What would you like me to do next?'
- 'What are the next steps?'
- 'When are you looking to start?'
- 'When would you like to meet again?'
- 'Have I answered all of your key questions today?'
- 'Shall we schedule a post proposal meeting in the diary?'
- 'Can you see any reason why we shouldn't move forward?'
- 'From your point of view, what are the next steps?'
- 'Realistically, when is the most practical time to start with this?'
- 'From a timing perspective, what makes this a particularly attractive or unattractive time to address this?'
- 'So does the whole proposal make sense to you?'
- 'So does everything look correct from your end?'
- 'So, I can set up delivery for next Tuesday or would Thursday be better?'
- 'We can meet so I can present our offer on Monday afternoon, or would you have more time later in the week?'
- 'Does the offer make sense?'
- 'Does that seem fair enough?'
- 'You had mentioned earlier that if everything looked right to you, then our next step would be XYZ. So first, does everything look right to you?'
- 'Great, so what's the best day for XYZ? Is Friday good or would next week be more convenient?'

- 'So have I answered all of your questions?'
- 'So how do you normally handle things like this from here?'
- 'Do you use purchase orders or do you usually just put things like this on a company card?'
- 'So, moving forward, will I work primarily with you as my main contact?'
- 'So, what do you say?'
- 'So, are you ready to start saving money today?'
- 'So, are you ready to begin earning more on your portfolio now?'
- 'So, I know your employees are ready to start enjoying the new work area, are you?'
- 'Are you ready to start today?'
- 'So, are you ready to let me go to work for you?'
- 'So, are you ready for us to start working for your organisation now?'
- 'So, how does that look to you?'
- 'Are you prepared to move forward?'
- 'Is your firm ready to go to the next level?'
- 'So, are you ready to partner with us on this?'

Account
management

To be honest, I could write a whole book on this section alone and, if I get the time, I will. Whatever industry you're in, however long your sales cycle is, and whatever your role is; whether a business development manager (BDM) or a strategic account manager, you need to manage the relationship as you would a new life partner. In fact, I know some sales people who have a better relationship with their client than they do with their partner, but that's yet another book.

Ultimately, you need to be their 'trusted advisor', and in some ways, this can be the scary fun part, a bit like the dating game we discussed earlier. Getting to know someone is interesting, but with your prospects, you will dig deep into every intimate part of their business. To be their trusted advisor, or partner, you need to know what makes them tick. More importantly, you need to know what keeps them awake at night.

I've tried not to use anecdotes, or 'When I was….' tales, but to illustrate the trusted advisor comment I will. When I worked for a UK telecoms giant, my client was the biggest regional and national TV broadcaster, with fingers in lots of pies. I partnered with them for nearly three years, helping with their blue-sky thinking, including the launch of a brand-new revenue stream, and upgrading their technology and infrastructure. By the end of year one, I didn't quite get to the 'staff security pass', but they did give me a hot desk I could work from. Yes, this can be normal with an implant, i.e., a techie delivering something, but not a sales guy, they trusted me. Building relationships with your existing customers is vital to achieve this, and you can do this in a number of ways, not least of all your day-to-day dealings with them, as well as formal account reviews.

There will be times when you need to sit down with each other and have a conversation about how well the account is being managed and the performance of the products and services. This is an ideal opportunity for you to understand more about them and their company to see if there are any other ways in which you can help and support them with their goals.

Never promise anything you can't deliver, underdelivering will not make you friends.

The Questions

- 'What could we have done better this year/period?'
- 'How did we do this year?'
- 'In what ways can we (I) improve?'
- 'What changes do we (I) need to make to ensure greater success?'
- 'What have we done well this year/period?'
- 'Has anything changed since we last met?'
- 'We haven't heard from you in a while. Did we do something wrong?' (If customer is dormant)

- 'If you could change one thing about our relationship, what would it be?'
- 'What goals would you like to see us (me) accomplish with you in the next 12 months?'
- 'What are your goals for next year compared with this year?'
- 'How's business?'
- 'How else can we help?'
- 'What are the organisation's upcoming goals?'
- 'Are you going to open any new offices/locations this year?'

Remember that any major change in the account presents the possibility that may open the door for more business. Also, the more you know about your clients' plans, the better you are able to be in position
to be of assistance.

- 'Are you recruiting any new employees at the moment?'
- 'Please don't just look at me as your (solution specific provider); I'm here to help in any number of ways. I have a vast array of contacts and may be of service in areas other than (solution specific). Are there any other areas which you need help with at the moment?'
- 'So that I can better be of assistance going forward, let me ask you a few questions: What is your long-term vision for the department?'
- 'In what other areas could this same problem occur?'

- 'How do we ensure that problems like this never happen again?'
- 'How can I better help you gain an advantage over your competition?'
- 'What would make your job easier? Maybe I can help with them, maybe I can't. However, I will better understand how I could be of help to you'

Clarifying questions

It may seem obvious, but asking your prospect clarification questions throughout the whole sales process fulfils two objectives:

1. They ensure your understanding of what the prospect has said is correct, reducing misunderstanding
2. They reassure the prospect that you are listening, you're interested in them and you are attempting to understand their requirements.

They are, therefore, critical questions that you need to master, and you might regard them as closed questions. If you have understood the point they have made, you need to paraphrase, summarise, confirm and demonstrate that you understand. A one-word positive answer in this situation is a good outcome, consequently, the quality of your listening skills will to a large extent determine your ultimate fate!

I haven't got a body language section in this book, but demonstrating active listening skills, with well-timed clarification questions is far more effective than just nodding your head throughout the meeting.

The Questions

- 'Am I right in assuming that all of your team will need training in how to use the system? Is that right?'
- 'So, let me double check. What we want to do is (Enter in here) Do I have it right?'
- 'Let me just make sure we're both on the same page (Enter in here) Does that sound like I've got it?'
- 'So just to confirm, you'd like to take the full package option with the platinum upgrade. Is that correct?'
- 'Okay, just to summarise your requirements then, you'll looking for an IT system to replace your existing one that will be more reliable with automatic monitoring dashboards so you're notified of problems instead of you finding out the hard way with downtime. Is that right?'
- 'So, the way I understand it is that what you really need to accomplish is (Enter in here), is that right?'
- 'Let me make sure I'm hearing you right. You want to shorten the overall hours your north store is open, plus (Enter in here) do I have that right?'
- 'Let me see if I am clear on this (Enter in here) am I on the same page with you?'
- 'I just want to make sure we are together on this. (Enter in here) does that sound like we're together?'

- 'Just to make sure I'm understanding you right (Enter in here) Have I got that right?'
- 'Let me make sure I get the idea. (Enter in here) is that right?'
- 'The way I see it is that (Enter in here) Is that the way you see it?'
- 'So just to make sure there is no confusion…

R h e t o r i c a l q u e s t i o n s

Rhetoric is the art of persuasion, whether through writing or through speech.

There are different types of rhetoric, for example Political Rhetoric. Examples of political rhetoric include political speeches that will often use rhetoric to evoke emotional responses in the audience. One famous example of this would of course be Martin Luther King, Jr.'s 'I Have a Dream' speech on 28th August 1963. His speech that day was delivered to 200,000 people, and was a vision that changed the world.

Therefore, rhetorical devices are techniques that are intended to help a speaker or an author to be effective in persuading his or her audience. In King's case, it persuaded President Lyndon B. Johnson's administration to push civil rights laws through the US congress. (See bibliography for wiki source).

And of course, if you're British and reading this, I can't discuss rhetorical questions without including Winston Churchill. Unbelievably, not only was he a great orator, he wrote and published over 1,000,000 more words than Charles Dickens. Who knew?

So, a rhetorical question is a device used to persuade or subtly influence the audience, or your customer. It's a question asked not for the answer, but for the effect. Sometimes, a rhetorical question is used to emphasise a point or just to get your customer or the audience thinking.

If this is applied to a sales scenario, rhetorical questions are asked to keep your prospects engaged. It also helps them to be more creative and come up with ideas.

The Questions

- 'Do you like to save money?'
- 'Do you like to make more money?'
- 'Do you like saving time and being more productive?'
- 'Isn't this a fantastic offer?'
- 'You want to close more sales, don't you?'
- 'You want to get more web traffic, don't you?'
- 'Isn't this work perfect?'
- 'Don't you like the way this package is set up?'
- 'Does that look good or what?'
- 'Do you want to do XYZ faster or slower?'
- 'Do you want to be more efficient or less efficient?'
- 'You want to stop losing money, don't you?'
- 'You want to get more business in the door, isn't that right?'

- 'This will give you much higher conversion/closing rates and that's the main thing you want, isn't it?'
- 'Do you want to outshine your competition?'
- 'If you had the power to (benefits of your solution) you would use it wouldn't you?'
- 'If you could (benefits of your solution) right now, would you?'
- 'Do you want to save time or waste time?'
- 'When is the best time to start saving money?'
- 'If I save you £X over the next month, would you call me for more?'
- 'How many times do you want to earn a huge bonus?'
- 'Do you really want to be the best in the business?'

Questions for getting referrals

Referrals are among the top ways' sales people get warm leads and new business, but many sales people struggle with generating them consistently. You have to know how to ask for them!

I'm sure you'll agree, it's so much easier to ring up a prospect and say,

'Hi Peter, John asked me to give you a call, he's just saved a load of money in his department and thinks I might be able to do the same for yours. I'm seeing him next week; can I pop in and see you for half an hour whilst I'm over there?'

If you've built up the rapport stage successfully at the start of the process, you'll know that many of your buyers rely on colleagues, associates and friends to recommend new suppliers or partners. So, when a prospect comes to us via this route, some of the hard yards are have already been done for us. Referrals build a salespersons trustworthiness and credibility—which are two of the main cornerstones of effective selling.

We all recognise the importance and the power of referrals; we don't always know how to tap into our client base or our networks to proactively generate sales referrals. This happens for a number of reasons. Many sales people are uncomfortable asking for referrals. They either don't want to appear 'salesy' or desperate for the work. Or it might be insecurity—they're not sure if they actually deliver value and benefit to their clients, and more generally because they have no idea about what to say as well as how to say it.

So, if you become skilled at getting referrals from your existing client base, your prospecting workload, with its stress and headaches will continually to decrease as your income or revenue increases.
Not to mention a pipeline that will be bursting at the seams!
Getting referrals is a main key to success.

The Questions

- 'Since you are so pleased with our work, would you recommend us to your peers?'

- 'I'm glad you're happy with what we've achieved. Who else in your network might need the same services?'
- 'How many of your peers can I also help to…?'
- 'Who else do you know that might also want to…?'
- 'XYZ is a huge company. Is there anyone else internally that might be interested in what we do?'
- 'I'm glad you love the product, John. Who else do you know who would benefit from it as well?'
- 'As you can see, what I do is help people with (benefits of solution). Off the top of your head, who do you know that might also benefit from this type of information/product/service?'
- 'The problem we solved for you is one that most people in your industry suffer from. Do you know of anyone else who I could help with this too?'
- 'I'm really glad that you're pleased with our work. I'd really appreciate it if you'd pass my name along to anyone else you know who would be interested in (what you do)'
- 'I'm really glad that you're pleased with our work. I'm always looking for referrals and wonder if you know anyone else who might be interested in…'

Other tactical sales tools

Throughout this book, I've tried to keep my narrative simple and written in plain English. I've also tried to reduce acronyms, and avoid business and 'busy' language that make things sound more important or complicated than they actually are.

You've asked the right questions, and you've got all the answers; i.e., you know who makes the decision, you know why they want to buy a new product, you know where the pain and pinch points are, what now?
Once you've gathered all the information you now need to position your solution so that it meets your customers' needs and desires, so it has to be put back to them in a language they understand, usually their own language.
The natural progression from the questioning stage is the demonstration or presentation of the offer, and the way to deliver this is through the structure of the Sales Value Proposition (SVP).

What is a Sales Value Proposition (SVP)?

A Sales Value Proposition (SVP) is a summary of how your product or service will benefit your customers.
A compelling SVP is the reason why a prospect will buy

from you and not your competitors. After your information gathering stage has finished, a well-crafted SVP that solves your customer's problem or satisfies their need is the next step. Each SVP consists of a selected bundle of products and/or services that caters to the requirements of a specific customer. In this sense, your SVP is a combination of benefits that your company offers customers. Some Sales Value Propositions (SVP) may be innovative and represent a new or disruptive offer. Others may be similar to existing market offers, but with added features, benefits and attributes.

Selling is all about helping a prospect make the decision to make a change. An SVP is one tool that salespeople should use to effectively communicate the value of the product or service that they are selling.

I draw a distinct line between what we do as salespeople and what comes out of our marketing departments, consequently I use the term Sales Value Proposition because rarely do salespeople use the value propositions that are generated by their marketing departments. Salespeople tend to shape the corporate value proposition into a format and into wording that is easier for them to express and is easily understood by their prospects.

Marketing may not like this, but it's a fact of life that a salesperson will mould a value proposition into a proposal that they feel is bespoke to their prospects and to a specific sector.

What an SVP isn't

An enticement

The word enticement is defined as a 'something used to attract or to tempt someone; a lure', and is designed to incentivise a prospect to act right away. Incentives are not value propositions, but often salespeople confuse them.

A tagline

A slogan or tagline is 'a catchphrase or small group of words that are combined in a special way to identify a product or company.' Slogans are not value propositions, but many salespeople confuse them.

It's not a positioning statement

A positioning statement is an expression of how a given product, service or brand fills a particular consumer need in a way that their competitors don't. A positioning statement is a subset of a value proposition, but it's not the same thing.

A strong SVP is vital

A good SVP that is communicated well, will quickly

focus potential customers on the main benefits i.e., improved ROI that your solution or service has to offer. Most customers already know what they're looking for even before the first meeting, so, if it's not clear at the start that your company can meet their needs, the sale won't progress.

If you've asked the right questions, and addressed the needs at the beginning, the SVP will create a strong differential between you and your competitors. An effective SVP will explain to the prospect why they should buy from you and not from the competition, and demonstrates not only your USP but how it meets their needs.

A company's generic value proposition targets your company's ideal customer and explains why your solution is the best option. This increases your chances of attracting the right prospects for your business and finding higher quality leads, but a bespoke SVP designed after you've put in the hard yards and asked the right questions, is more likely to convert the prospect to a customer.

A strong SVP provides clarity and makes it immediately clear to your customers what your offer is. Done correctly, a Sales Value Proposition can give your business a huge advantage over your competitors, but very few businesses have one, in fact a recent study shows;
'Only 2.2% of companies have effective Sales Value Propositions.' Clearly this is a huge problem but gives you, the reader, a distinct advantage because an ineffective value proposition that takes a shot gun approach can make your ideal customers turn to the competition simply because they don't immediately understand that your product meets their needs. I've been on the coalface so I know how challenging it is to distil your company's services down into one or two sentences. which is why I decided to add in this section.

Things to consider

What is it you're selling?

Make sure you take into account the point of view of your target audience and explain your services in their language and in a way that will appeal to them. Even if you offer exactly what they're looking for, if it isn't worded in a way that makes that clear, potential customers will look elsewhere. Think about your prospect's needs, and make sure your SVP meets their needs as closely as possible. Consider what your customers are looking for and how they phrase their needs, and reuse this phrasing into your proposal.

"KEEP THE FOCUS ON YOUR AUDIENCE BENEFITS"

Make sure the focus is on how your services will benefit your audience. Include specific metrics if possible. For example, have your customers seen an average percent increase in revenue? Do they save a certain number of hours per week? Have they reported an increase in performance since starting to use your services?

Who are you selling to?

Before you start writing your value proposition you will want to be perfectly clear on who your target audience is. To accomplish this, research your audience to understand who they are and what they look for in products or services like yours.

You'll want to have answers to the following questions:

'WHO ARE THEY AND WHAT THEY DO?

'WHAT ARE THEIR VALUES?'

'WHAT ARE THEIR NEEDS OR PAIN POINTS?'

'WHAT CHALLENGES DID THEY EXPERIENCE BEFORE WORKING WITH YOU?'

'WHAT MOTIVATED THEM TO SEARCH FOR WHAT YOU OFFER?'

'WAS THERE ANYTHING ABOUT YOUR PARTICULAR SOLUTION THAT SHOWED THAT YOU CATERED TO THEIR NEEDS?'

Once you've answered these types of questions you can start to develop an accurate customer profile that you can tailor your SVP to.

What is your differentiator?

It's essential that your SVP includes a unique selling point or feature that sets your company apart. Let's face it, you have competitors all offering similar products or services, so how do you differentiate? Most of your potential customers will compare their options, so you will need to convince them that you are different and better than all the other suppliers.

Even if you already have an idea of your differentiating factors, it's a good idea to spend some time doing some competitor analysis. The best way to go about doing this is by checking out their sites and examining their marketing campaigns.

Then ask yourself the following questions:

'WHAT ARE YOUR COMPETITORS LACKING?'

'WHAT DO YOU DO BETTER THAN THEM?'

'WHY DO THESE DIFFERENCES MATTER TO YOUR CUSTOMERS?'

Once you have clear answers to these questions, you can begin to write a more effective value proposition.

Effective SVP's and their impact on your conversion rates.

A good value proposition can make all the difference in your sales conversions and, as a result, revenue. Similarly, a weak value proposition can result in poor sales.

What makes an effective SVP?

A really good SVP summarises what your company does in one sentence, however, for maximum impact and to articulate what your company does in a single sentence, your value proposition needs to be both clear, concise and credible.

Clear because it's specific about the benefits, concise because it uses limited narrative and credible because it delivers the right benefits to your customers' expectations.

An effective SVP should also show how you solve a specific problem or address a specific need, and it should also be clear on what problem or need you are resolving, and finally it needs to demonstrate how you solve this problem.

One of the most important steps is to demonstrate how customers in similar industries or sectors choose your offer over your competitors and it needs to clearly and compellingly explain why. However, under no circumstance does your SVP include wild exaggerations, that make statements that you can't prove i.e. 'Our plasterboards are the best insulated in the market'. What you can say with the right metrics is, 'Our plasterboards can reduce your heating costs by 30%.'

If you have an SVP, be honest and ask yourself the following questions:

IS YOUR SVP CLEAR?

DO YOU ADDRESS A NEED?

DOES IT SHOW CLEAR RESULTS WITH A SIMILAR CLIENT?

How to write a compelling SVP

Keep it straightforward

Many businesses make the mistake of using buzz words or wishy-washy language that all of their competitors are using, like 'results-driven solutions'. Phrases like these don't solve the customers problem and doesn't help you to stand out in the market place. When crafting your SVP, use your customers language or acronyms, be clear on what you are offering and avoid YOUR industry jargon or acronyms.

Make it stand out

Most of your potential customers will read several other companies' value propositions in the course of the buying cycle. That's why it's extremely important for you to make sure they remember yours by your use of your SVP content. To make your company stand out do a little Googling on your competitors to see what they're offering. You can then develop and highlight the USP's of your offer and differentiate you from those of your competitors.

Emphasise your added value

As the name implies, your SVP needs to convey the value of what your solution delivers to the prospect. Although your differentiator may be around the clock support, it's more important to highlight how your solution helps them to achieve a specific goal.

The top attributes
for an effective SVP

To build on those three core areas, I'm going to dig a little deeper into the key attributes necessary to attract the prospects attention and accelerate the buyer's decision-making process. Your SVP must be:

Distinct

As well as being clear and concise as we discussed above, the value your solution can create should be blindingly obvious to the prospect, if you achieve this it will also show it will create value for them. This is the eureka moment when the prospect can visualise the approximate value they will receive from your product or service. This is why your SVP must be expressed in terms and language that are familiar to your prospect so that they can quickly understand its relevance and value.

Flexible

One central aspect that your SVP must address is that your product or service can integrate with the customers' existing processes. This doesn't mean that some of their processes won't be affected or change. But at the level of a first contact, the potential prospect must be assured that buying and implementing your product or service won't disrupt their entire company.

Scalable

A sales value proposition should address scalability
and relate how your solution and the value it provides
meet the future needs of the customer. Customers rarely
say 'I just want a solution that solves today's problem.'

Your SVP needs to demonstrate the value and the ROI,
that is delivered by your solution. You can address this
most effectively in your SVP with metrics gathered from
referenceable current customers. 'Other customers of ours
who implemented this solution averaged a 30% decrease
in waste.'

Your final slide can combine several or all of the points
above and could read something like 'Our customers on
average experience a 30% reduction in waste (defendable)
within the first 12 months and a 40% reduction over the
first 3 years of usage (scalable).'

T y p e s   o f   S V P ' s

Your SVP creates value for a specific prospect
through a bespoke mix of all the elements discussed above
to address their needs. The value might be quantitative
(i.e. a price, cost reduction or faster delivery) or
qualitative (i.e. a more intuitive interface or enhanced
customer experience).
Components from the following list can contribute to
the 'value add' you build for the customer, and then of
course you'll think of your own.

Price

Offering similar value at a lower price is a common way to satisfy the needs of price-sensitive customers. No frills airlines, such as easyJet and Ryanair have designed entire business models specifically to enable low-cost air travel. Another example of a price-based Value Proposition can be seen in the Nano, a new car designed and manufactured by the Indian conglomerate Tata. Its surprisingly low price makes the automobile affordable to a whole new segment of the Indian population. Increasingly, free offers are starting to permeate various industries. Free offers range from free newspapers to free e-mail, free mobile phone services and more.

Performance

Improving product or service performance has traditionally been a common way to create value. The IT sector has traditionally relied on this factor by bringing more powerful devices and machines to market. But improved performance has its limits. In recent years, for example, faster PCs, more disk storage space and better graphics have failed to produce corresponding growth in customer demand.

Cost reduction

Helping customers reduce costs is an important way to create value. Hubspot, for example, sells a hosted Customer Relationship management (CRM) application. This relieves buyers from the expense and trouble of having to buy, install and manage CRM software themselves.

Risk reduction

Customer's value reducing the risks they incur when purchasing products or services. For a used car buyer, a one-year service guarantee reduces the risk of post-purchase breakdowns and repairs. A service-level agreement (SLA) partially reduces the risk undertaken by a purchaser of outsourced IT services.

Bespoke

Tailoring products and services to the specific needs of individual customers or Customer Segments creates value. In recent years, the concepts of mass customisation and customer co-creation have gained importance. This approach allows for customised
products and services, while still taking advantage of economies of scale.

Design
Design is an important but difficult element to measure. A product like iPhone packaging may stand out because of superior design, in fact many other non-tech industries are copying it. In the fashion,
furniture and consumer electronics industries, design can be a particularly important part of your SVP.

Branding

Customers may find value in the simple act of using and displaying a specific brand. Driving a Bentley signifies wealth, for example. On the other end of the spectrum, rugby supporters might wear 'Oddballs' accessories like hats and scarves to show they support a testicular cancer charity.

Availability

Making products and services available to customers who previously lacked access to them is another way to create value. This can result from business model innovation, new technologies, or a combination of both. See UBA. Using an innovative business model, UBA offers cheap, almost instant access to private cabs, a service previously unaffordable to a range of some customers.

Blue Sky

Some SVPs satisfy an entirely new set of needs that customers previously didn't perceive because there was no similar offering. This is often, but not always, technology related. Cell phones for instance, created a whole new industry around mobile communication. On the other hand, products such as ethical investment funds have little to do with new
technology.

Intuitive

Making things more convenient or easier to use can create substantial value. Back in the day with iPod and iTunes, Apple offered customers unprecedented convenience searching, buying, downloading, and listening to digital music. It now dominates the market.

In Closing

Targeted, well written Sales Value Propositions will not only help you close on specific deals but will also help your business attract new customers in the same sector. This is easier said than done, as developing a compelling Sales Value Proposition is challenging. In this book, I've highlighted key practices that can help you write or improve a Sales Value Proposition, as well as some real time highly effective ones.

In short, you want to keep the language clear, concise, and specifically targeted at your customer so there's no ambiguity in what sets you apart from the competition. You need to demonstrate value with compelling metrics and you need to demonstrate that you are solving problems with your product. If you follow these guidelines, you have a so much better chance of developing an SVP that is effective and helps you to convert more prospects into trading customers.

An example SVP might look like this:

Super Saver Software

- **Headline:** 'Save Time and Money with Super Saver Software - The Ultimate Solution for Efficient Budgeting and Expense Management'
- **Problem or need:** Many individuals and businesses struggle with effectively managing their budgets and controlling expenses. This often leads to financial stress, overspending and inefficient processes.
- **Solution:** Super Saver Software offers a user-friendly and comprehensive platform that simplifies budgeting and expense management. Our software is designed to streamline financial tasks, providing an all-in-one solution that saves you time and money.
- **Key benefits and value:**
- Easily accessible: Our software features an intuitive graphical user interface (GUI) that can be used by anyone in your organisation, regardless of their level of financial expertise.
- Cost savings: With Super Saver Software, you can reduce unnecessary expenses by up to 30%, helping you optimise your budget and maximise your savings.
- Integration capabilities: Our software seamlessly integrates with existing systems, allowing for

smooth data transfer and eliminating the need for complex manual processes.

- Cross-platform compatibility: Whether you're using a Mac OS or Windows, Super Saver Software works seamlessly on both platforms, ensuring flexibility and convenience.
- **Proof or evidence:** Hear what our satisfied customers have to say:
- 'Since implementing Super Saver Software, we have significantly reduced our monthly expenses and gained better control over our budget. It's a game-changer!' - John Smith, CEO of XYZ Company.
- 'The user-friendly interface of Super Saver Software has made budgeting a breeze for our entire team. We've seen tangible cost savings and improved financial efficiency.' - Sarah Johnson, CFO of ABC Corporation.
- **Call to action:** Start saving time and money today! Sign up for a free trial of Super Saver Software or contact our sales team to schedule a personalised demo and learn how our solution can transform your budgeting and expense management processes.

The Summary

Euripides 'Question everything.
Learn something. Answer Nothing'

Yes, before you write to me, this is a picture of Einstein and not Euripides. Truth is, he did regurgitate a short version of Euripides above quote as 'Question Everything.' it's clearly very important if Einstein is involved, or is this plagerism his little skeleton in the cupboard?

However, he did say,
'The important thing is **not to stop questioning**. Curiosity **has** its own reason for existing. One cannot help but be in awe when he contemplates the mysteries of eternity, of life, of the marvellous structure of reality. It is enough if one tries merely to comprehend a little of this mystery every day.'

End Matter-Part One

No book about sales would be complete with at least a nodding reference to prospecting. Throughout this book I've assumed that the sales or business people have already done the hard yards and have managed to get in front of the prospect. Consequently, in this second edition, I thought it might be worth highlighting at least the important parts of the prospecting framework, but with the caveat, like 'Account Management' it could be a whole book on its own. The good news is that many of the questions included in this book can be applied to prospecting for new business.

During my sales career, I've worked in companies that operate different telesales prospecting structures including;

- Organisations that have a dedicated telesales department that work on a postcode territory basis. They blitz a patch and make appointments for the sales person on that patch. Luxury if you don't like prospecting.
- A company that had an outbound sales prospecting day once a week. All the sales people came into the office and the challenge was on. Whoever made the most appointments would win a bottle of champagne or something similar. This was also good team building and encouraged competitive camaraderie.

- I've worked for companies that focused on industries and verticals, and I've also made my own appointments either in my own postcodes or later on in my career in the Countries I was responsible for.

I believe sales people need to go through the baptism of fire doing cold calling to help build their sales resilience. I have no stats to back that up, just my own experience.

Prospecting

Here's a quick overview to the Client Prospecting process and then we'll go into each one in a bit more in-depth:

- Client prospecting is a fundamental skill for salespeople to drive business growth.
- It involves identifying and engaging potential clients or customers.
- Effective client prospecting is crucial for generating leads and increasing sales revenue.

Skills Required for Effective Client Prospecting:

- Active Listening
- Communication and Persuasion
- Resilience and Persistence

Methodologies for Client Prospecting:

Market Research:
- Thorough market research is essential for identifying the target audience and understanding their needs.
- Sales professionals can tailor their prospecting strategies based on market insights.

Networking:
- Building and nurturing professional networks is important for client prospecting.
- Attending industry events and leveraging online platforms can help establish connections and uncover leads.

Cold Calling:
- Cold calling involves reaching out to prospects who haven't expressed prior interest.
- Researching the prospect's business and personalising the conversation is crucial for successful cold calling.

Email Marketing:
- Leveraging targeted email campaigns is a powerful prospecting tool.
- Crafting compelling emails with a clear call-to-action can capture the attention of potential clients.

Social Media:
- Social media platforms offer opportunities for client prospecting.
- Engaging with potential clients, sharing relevant content, and participating in industry discussions can establish credibility.

Okay, so let's expand on those one by one, bearing in mind they are all crucial components of prospecting for new clients.

S w e e t   S p o t

Market research is the first crucial component of client prospecting as it helps sales professionals gather relevant information about the market, target audience and competitive landscape. By conducting comprehensive market research, salespeople can make informed decisions, refine their prospecting strategies and maximise their chances of success.

Key areas are:

- Identifying Target Market: The first step in market research is identifying the target market or audience for the company's products or services. Sales professionals need to understand who their potential customers are, their characteristics, demographics and specific needs. This information helps in narrowing down the prospecting efforts and tailoring the messaging to resonate with the target audience.
- Market Size and Growth Potential: It's important to assess the size of the market and its growth potential. This involves analysing industry reports, market studies and data sources to gather information about the overall market size, trends and projections. Understanding the market's growth potential helps salespeople assess the opportunities available and prioritise their prospecting efforts accordingly.
- Competitor Analysis: Analysing the competitive landscape is crucial to identify competitors, their

offerings and market positioning. Sales professionals need to understand their competitors' strengths, weaknesses, pricing strategies and unique selling propositions. This knowledge helps in positioning the company's products or services effectively, highlighting differentiators, and addressing any gaps or shortcomings in the market.

- Customer Needs and Preferences: Market research involves gaining insights into customer needs, pain points and preferences. Sales professionals can use surveys, interviews, or focus groups to gather direct feedback from potential customers. Understanding their needs and preferences allows salespeople to customise their prospecting approaches and emphasise the benefits that resonate most with the target audience.

- Market Trends and Opportunities: Staying updated on industry trends, technological advancements and emerging opportunities is crucial for effective prospecting. Sales professionals need to monitor industry publications, attend conferences or trade shows, and engage with industry experts to gather insights into the latest developments. By staying informed, salespeople can identify new niches, evolving customer demands, or untapped market segments for their prospecting efforts.

- Distribution Channels and Partnerships: Understanding the existing distribution channels and potential partnership opportunities can significantly impact prospecting strategies. Sales professionals should explore the current distribution networks, identify potential partners or influencers and assess the feasibility of collaborations. Leveraging existing channels or forming strategic partnerships can help reach a wider audience and generate more qualified leads.

- Regulatory and Legal Considerations: Market research should also encompass an understanding of relevant regulations and legal considerations that may impact prospecting efforts. Sales professionals need to be aware of any industry-specific regulations, compliance requirements, or licensing procedures to ensure that their prospecting activities align with the legal framework.

- By conducting thorough market research, sales professionals can gather valuable insights about their target market, competitors, customer needs and emerging opportunities. This knowledge empowers them to develop effective prospecting strategies, tailor their messaging and approach potential clients with a deep understanding of their unique requirements. Ultimately, market research enhances the chances of success in client prospecting and helps sales teams achieve their goals.

N e t w o r k i n g

Networking is another crucial aspect of client prospecting that involves building and nurturing relationships with individuals and organisations within
your industry or target market. Effective networking

allows sales professionals to expand their reach, establish trust and uncover potential client opportunities. Key requirements are:

- Building a Professional Network: Building a professional network involves connecting with individuals who can potentially become clients, referral sources or industry influencers. This can be done through various avenues such as attending industry events, conferences, trade shows, and joining professional organisations or networking groups. Building a network enables sales professionals to establish relationships with key decision-makers and gain visibility within their target market.
- Establishing Trust and Credibility: Networking provides an opportunity to establish trust and credibility with potential clients. By engaging in meaningful conversations, sharing knowledge, and offering assistance or insights, sales professionals can position themselves as trusted advisors and experts in their field. Building trust is essential for successful client prospecting as it increases the likelihood of referrals, recommendations and, ultimately, new business opportunities.
- Leveraging Existing Connections: Networking allows sales professionals to leverage their existing connections to expand their reach. By tapping into the networks of colleagues, friends, or industry contacts, salespeople can gain introductions or referrals to potential clients. Existing connections can provide valuable insights, warm introductions, and endorsements that help in

initiating conversations and building relationships with potential clients.

- Online Networking: In today's digital age, online networking has become increasingly important. Utilising social media platforms, professional networking sites, and online communities can significantly expand your reach and provide opportunities to connect with potential clients. Engaging in discussions, sharing valuable content, and participating in relevant online groups or forums can help establish your presence, attract attention, and initiate conversations with potential clients.

- Follow-Up and Relationship Nurturing: Effective networking involves consistent follow-up and relationship nurturing. After initial meetings or interactions, it's important to follow up promptly and maintain regular communication with potential clients. This can be done through personalised emails, phone calls, or arranging follow-up meetings. By staying on their radar and nurturing the relationship over time, sales professionals can increase the chances of converting potential clients into actual customers.

- Offering Value: Networking is not just about seeking opportunities for yourself but also about offering value to others. By providing assistance, sharing industry insights, or making relevant introductions, sales professionals can position themselves as valuable resources to their network. This reciprocity builds goodwill, strengthens relationships, and encourages others to reciprocate by referring potential clients or providing opportunities in return.

- Continuous Learning and Development: Networking provides an opportunity to learn from others and stay updated on industry trends, challenges and best practices. Engaging in conversations, attending industry events, and actively seeking knowledge from industry experts or thought leaders can help sales professionals stay ahead of the curve. Continuous learning and development not only enhance your expertise but also enable you to provide valuable insights and solutions to potential clients.

Networking is a dynamic and ongoing process that requires time, effort and genuine interest in building meaningful connections. By effectively leveraging your network, establishing trust and offering value, you can significantly enhance your client prospecting efforts and open doors to new business opportunities.

Cold calling

Cold calling is a sales technique that involves reaching out to potential clients or customers who have had no prior contact or relationship with the salesperson. It typically involves making unsolicited phone calls to introduce products or services, initiate conversations, and generate interest in the hopes of setting up a meeting or closing a sale. Key points are:

- Targeted Prospecting: Before engaging in cold calling, it's crucial to identify and target the right audience. This involves conducting thorough research to identify potential clients or companies that align with your product or service offering. By focusing on a specific target market or industry, you can increase the chances of success and tailor your approach accordingly.

- Developing a Script or Framework: Cold calling requires preparation to ensure a clear and concise message. Developing a script or framework helps sales professionals stay focused, deliver a compelling pitch and handle potential objections. While it's important to have a structure in place, it's equally essential to maintain a conversational tone and be flexible to adapt based on the prospect's responses.

- Value Proposition: When cold calling, it's crucial to communicate a strong value proposition that clearly outlines the benefits or solutions your product or service offers. Highlighting how your offering addresses the prospect's pain points or improves their situation is key to capturing their interest. Tailoring your value proposition to each prospect based on their specific needs or challenges can significantly enhance the effectiveness of your cold calls.

- Building Rapport: Establishing rapport and building a connection with the prospect is essential in cold calling. It's important to approach the call with a friendly and professional tone, actively listening to the prospect's responses, and showing genuine interest in their needs or concerns. Building rapport helps create a positive impression, gain trust, and increase the likelihood of a meaningful conversation.

- Handling Objections: Cold calling often involves encountering objections from prospects. It's important to be prepared to address common objections effectively and confidently. By understanding the prospect's concerns and offering relevant solutions or information, you can overcome objections and keep the conversation progressing.
- Persistence and Follow-Up: Cold calling requires persistence and a willingness to follow up. Not all prospects will be ready to make a decision or engage in a conversation immediately. By maintaining a consistent follow-up strategy, such as scheduling future calls or sending personalised follow-up emails, you increase the chances of converting prospects into customers over time.
- Continuous Improvement: Cold calling is a skill that can be continuously improved through practice and self-reflection.
Analysing your cold calling efforts, identifying areas for improvement, and seeking feedback from colleagues or managers can help refine your approach and enhance your success rate.
- Compliance and Etiquette: It's important to adhere to legal and ethical guidelines when cold calling. Familiarise yourself with relevant regulations, such as Do Not Call lists, and ensure you comply with them. Additionally, practicing good telephone etiquette, such as introducing yourself politely, respecting the prospect's time and being professional throughout the call, helps create a

positive impression and fosters productive conversations.

Cold calling can be a challenging and sometimes unpredictable sales technique, but with proper preparation, a strong value proposition and a focus on building rapport, it can be an effective method for generating leads, setting up meetings and closing sales.

E m a i l   m a r k e t i n g

Email marketing is a digital marketing strategy that involves sending targeted, personalised emails to a group of individuals or subscribers with the aim of promoting products, services, or engaging with the audience. It is a widely used marketing technique that offers several benefits. Key points are:

- Building an Email List: The first step in email marketing is to build a list of subscribers who have willingly provided their email addresses and given consent to receive communications from your business. This can be done through various methods such as website sign-up forms, lead generation campaigns, or opt-in incentives like free resources or exclusive offers. Building a quality email list is essential for effective email marketing.
- Segmentation and Personalisation: Once you have an email list, segmenting your subscribers based on various criteria allows you to send targeted and relevant content. By categorising subscribers based

on factors like demographics, purchase history, or interests, you can tailor your email campaigns to specific segments, increasing the chances of engagement and conversion. Personalisation goes beyond addressing recipients by their names—it involves delivering content that speaks to their specific needs, preferences or past interactions with your business.

- Crafting Compelling Email Content: Creating engaging and persuasive email content is crucial for successful email marketing. Your emails should have a clear objective, whether it's promoting a product, sharing educational content, announcing a sale or nurturing customer relationships. The content should be concise, well-written and visually appealing, incorporating elements like images, videos, and call-to-action buttons to encourage recipients to take the desired action.

- Automation and Drip Campaigns: Email marketing tools and platforms offer automation features that allow you to set up pre-defined email sequences or drip campaigns. These campaigns can be triggered by specific actions or events, such as a new subscriber joining your list or a customer making a purchase. Drip campaigns help nurture leads and guide them through the customer journey by delivering a series of targeted emails over a specified period. Automation saves time, ensures consistency, and helps deliver timely and relevant content to your subscribers.

- A/B Testing and Optimisation: To improve the effectiveness of your email campaigns, it's important to conduct A/B tests. This involves creating two variations of an email with slight differences in elements like subject lines, call-to-action buttons, or content layout. By analysing the performance of these variations, you can determine which elements resonate better with your audience and optimise future campaigns accordingly. Continuous testing and optimisation help enhance open rates, click-through rates, and overall engagement.

- Monitoring Metrics and Analytics: Email marketing provides valuable data and analytics to measure the success of your campaigns. Key metrics to monitor include open rates, click-through rates, conversion rates, bounce rates and unsubscribe rates. By analysing these metrics, you can gain insights into the effectiveness of your emails, identify areas for improvement, and make data-driven decisions to optimise future campaigns.

- Compliance and Subscriber Consent: When conducting email marketing, it's important to comply with applicable laws and regulations, such as the General Data Protection Regulation (GDPR) in Europe or the CAN-SPAM Act in the United States. Ensure that you have proper consent from subscribers to send them marketing emails and include a clear option to unsubscribe in every email. Respecting subscribers' privacy and providing a seamless unsubscribe process is crucial for maintaining a positive brand image and building trust.

- Continuous Engagement and Relationship Building: Email marketing is not just about promoting products or services; it's an opportunity to build lasting relationships with your audience. Regularly engaging with your subscribers by delivering valuable content, exclusive offers, or personalised recommendations helps establish trust, loyalty and brand advocacy. Encouraging two-way communication by inviting feedback or responding to customer inquiries further strengthens the relationship.

Email marketing remains a powerful and cost-effective marketing tool that allows businesses to reach their audience directly and deliver tailored messages. By employing segmentation, personalisation, automation, and continuous optimisation, you can leverage email marketing to drive engagement, conversions and long-term customer loyalty.

Social media

Social media refers to online platforms and websites that enable users to create, share and interact with content in a virtual community. Social media has become an integral part of people's lives, and it has also transformed the way businesses approach marketing and customer engagement.

Here's an expanded explanation of social media:

- Platform Diversity: Social media encompasses a wide range of platforms, each with its own unique features and user base. Some of the most popular social media platforms include Facebook,

Instagram, Twitter (X), LinkedIn, YouTube, Pinterest
and TikTok. Each platform attracts a different demographic and offers various content formats, such as text, images, videos, live streaming, stories and more. Understanding the characteristics and audience of each platform is essential for developing an effective social media strategy.

- Brand Presence and Profile: Businesses can establish their brand presence on social media platforms by creating profiles or pages that represent their business. These profiles act as a hub where businesses can share information, interact with their audience and showcase their products, services, or expertise. It's important to optimize these profiles with accurate and compelling descriptions, relevant keywords, and high-quality visuals to make a strong first impression and attract followers.

- Content Creation and Sharing: Social media revolves around content creation and sharing. Businesses can leverage social media platforms to create and distribute various types of content, including articles, blog posts, images, videos, infographics, podcasts and more. The content should be tailored to the platform and aligned with the interests and preferences of the target audience. Sharing valuable and engaging content helps businesses attract followers, increase brand awareness and foster engagement.

- Community Building and Engagement: Social media provides an opportunity to build a community around your brand. By actively engaging with your audience through comments, likes, shares and direct messages, you can foster a sense of connection and loyalty. Responding to customer inquiries, addressing concerns, and acknowledging user-generated content helps build trust and a positive brand image. Encouraging user participation, such as running contests, polls, or interactive campaigns, further strengthens community engagement.

- Targeted Advertising: Social media platforms offer powerful advertising tools that allow businesses to target specific audiences based on demographics, interests, behaviours and more. Through targeted advertising, businesses can reach a larger audience beyond their existing followers and increase brand visibility. These platforms provide various ad formats, including sponsored posts, display ads, video ads, carousel ads and more, enabling businesses to create visually appealing and compelling advertisements.

- Influencer Marketing: Influencer marketing is a strategy that involves collaborating with influential individuals on social media to promote products, services or brand messages. Influencers have a loyal following and can help businesses tap into their audience and gain credibility. By partnering with influencers who align with your brand values and target audience, you can leverage their reach and influence to expand your brand's reach and generate buzz.

- Social Listening and Customer Insights: Social media provides businesses with a wealth of customer insights and feedback. By monitoring conversations, mentions and hashtags related to your brand or industry, you can gain valuable insights into customer preferences, sentiment and trends. This information can be used to improve products, tailor marketing strategies and enhance customer experience.

- Performance Analytics and Measurement: Social media platforms offer analytics and measurement tools to track the performance of your social media efforts. Metrics such as follower growth, reach, engagement rate, clicks, conversions and sentiment analysis can provide valuable insights into the effectiveness of your social media strategy. By analysing these metrics, you can identify successful tactics, optimise your content strategy, and make data-driven decisions to improve your social media presence.

Social media offers businesses a powerful platform to connect with their target audience, increase brand visibility, drive engagement and gather valuable insights. It's essential to develop a well-planned social media strategy that aligns with your business goals and audience preferences to effectively leverage the opportunities offered by social media.

T e l e s a l e s

Telesales is an effective prospecting method but, there are challenges associated with it:

- Telesales, or telephone sales, can be a highly effective prospecting method for reaching out to potential clients and generating new business opportunities. Here are some reasons why telesales can be an effective approach:
- Direct Communication: Telesales allows for direct and immediate communication with prospects. It enables you to engage in real-time conversations, build rapport, address objections and provide immediate responses to questions or concerns. This direct interaction can help you tailor your pitch and address the specific needs of each prospect, increasing the chances of conversion.
- Scalability: Telesales offers scalability, allowing you to reach a large number of prospects within a short period. With proper planning and organisation, you can efficiently target a wide audience and generate a higher volume of leads compared to other prospecting methods.
- Personalisation: Telesales allows for a personalised approach. By speaking directly with prospects, you can gather valuable insights about their needs, pain points, and preferences. This information enables you to tailor your message, positioning your products or services as a solution that directly addresses their specific challenges.
Immediate Feedback: Telesales provides immediate feedback from prospects. Through conversations, you can gauge their level of interest, identify objections or barriers to purchase and adjust your approach accordingly. This real-time feedback helps you refine your sales strategies and improve your prospecting techniques.

- Challenges in Telesales and the Importance of Adopting the Right Mindset and Being Targeted:
- Telesales, like any other prospecting method, comes with its own set of challenges. Here are some common challenges and why adopting the right mindset and being targeted is crucial:
- Rejection: Telesales professionals often face rejection. It's essential to have the right mindset to handle rejection positively and persistently. Understanding that rejection is a natural part of the sales process and maintaining a positive attitude can help you bounce back quickly and remain motivated.
- Gatekeepers: Dealing with gatekeepers, such as receptionists or assistants, can pose a challenge. These individuals often screen calls and may try to prevent access to decision-makers. By adopting a targeted approach and developing strategies to engage and build relationships with gatekeepers, you can increase your chances of reaching the intended decision-makers.
- Limited Attention Span: In today's fast-paced world, prospects have limited attention spans. Capturing their attention and effectively conveying your message within a short timeframe is crucial. Being concise, engaging and focused on the prospect's needs can help overcome this challenge and keep prospects interested in the conversation.
- Adapting to Different Personalities: Prospecting involves interacting with individuals who have different personalities, communication styles and preferences. Adapting your approach to accommodate these differences is vital for building

rapport and establishing a connection. Developing strong listening skills and being able to quickly assess and adjust to each prospect's style can help overcome this challenge.

- Targeting the Right Audience: One of the most critical aspects of telesales is targeting the right audience. Identifying your ideal customer profile and conducting thorough research can help ensure that you're reaching out to prospects who are most likely to have a genuine interest in your products or services. A targeted approach saves time and increases the chances of success.

- Continuous Learning and Improvement: Telesales requires ongoing learning and improvement. Staying updated on industry trends, refining your communication skills, and seeking feedback from prospects and colleagues are essential for enhancing your telesales effectiveness. Embracing a growth mindset and being open to feedback can help you adapt and improve your prospecting techniques over time.

Telesales can be an effective prospecting method, providing direct communication, scalability, personalisation and immediate feedback. However, it also comes with challenges, such as rejection, dealing with gatekeepers, limited attention spans, adapting to different personalities, targeting the right audience and the need for continuous learning and improvement. By adopting the right mindset, remaining targeted in your approach, and addressing these challenges proactively, you can increase your success in telesales prospecting

How important are Statistics in prospecting and for Business Growth?

When it comes to client prospecting, highlighting relevant statistics is a powerful way to capture the attention of potential clients and demonstrate the value and effectiveness of your products or services.

Here are some key statistics that are important to consider when prospecting:

- Market Size: Highlighting the size of the target market can showcase the potential opportunities for growth. This could include statistics such as the total number of potential customers, the market's annual revenue or its projected growth rate. Demonstrating a sizable and expanding market can attract clients who are looking to tap into new customer segments or capitalise on industry trends.
- Customer Demographics: Understanding the demographics of your target audience is crucial for effective prospecting. Presenting statistics related to your ideal customer profile, such as age, gender, location, income level or industry, can demonstrate that you have a deep understanding of your clients' needs and preferences. This helps build trust and credibility with potential clients.
Competitor Analysis: Providing statistics related to your competitors can highlight your unique selling

points and position your business as a valuable alternative. This could include data on market share, customer satisfaction ratings, pricing comparisons or customer testimonials. By demonstrating how your business outperforms competitors, you can showcase the advantages of choosing your products or services.

- Return on Investment (ROI): Showing potential clients the tangible benefits they can expect from investing in your products or services is crucial. Highlighting statistics related to ROI, such as cost savings, revenue growth or increased efficiency, can illustrate the potential value your offering brings to their business. Case studies or success stories that showcase measurable results can be particularly impactful.

- Customer Satisfaction and Testimonials: Sharing statistics related to customer satisfaction rates, positive feedback, or testimonials can help build trust and credibility. This could include data on customer retention rates, Net Promoter Score (NPS), or survey results. Positive testimonials from satisfied clients can serve as social proof and demonstrate the value and quality of your offerings.

- Industry Trends: Providing statistics related to industry trends can position your business as forward-thinking and up-to-date with the latest developments. This could include data on emerging technologies, consumer behaviour shifts or market predictions. By showcasing your knowledge of industry trends, you can position your business as a trusted advisor and demonstrate your ability to adapt to changing market dynamics.

- Success Stories: Sharing real-life success stories and case studies can be compelling for potential clients. Highlight statistics related to specific client achievements, such as revenue growth percentages, cost savings or increased customer engagement. By showcasing how your products or services have positively impacted other businesses, you provide concrete evidence of your ability to deliver results.
- Social Proof: Highlighting statistics related to your business's reputation and credibility can be influential. This could include the number of satisfied customers, awards or certifications received or positive media coverage. These statistics demonstrate that your business is well-regarded in the industry and can be trusted to deliver on its promises.
- When prospecting clients, it's important to tailor the statistics you highlight to their specific needs and pain points. By presenting relevant and compelling data, you can capture their attention, demonstrate the value of your offerings and increase the likelihood of securing new clients for business growth.

Client prospecting is an indispensable skill for sales professionals seeking to drive business growth. I personally love a challenge and it's one of my favourite parts of the sales process. By employing a combination of methodologies like market research, networking, cold calling, email marketing and social media outreach, salespeople can effectively identify and engage potential clients. Essential skills such as active listening, communication and persuasion, resilience and persistence contribute to successful prospecting efforts. The importance of client prospecting in business growth is supported by statistics that highlight its challenges and the impact it has on sales success.

Mastering the art of client prospecting empowers salespeople to expand their customer base, generate leads, and ultimately increase sales revenue, contributing to the overall success of a business.

PART 2

Curiouser and curiouser

Pascal's Wager
(1998)

*'Is it better to believe in God and it turns out to be
wrong? Or, is it better to be an atheist, and after you
die find out that God exists'?*

As human beings, we have an insatiable desire for
knowledge, and we can satisfy this hunger by asking
questions. In fact, asking questions is the most effective
way to acquire knowledge and gain a deeper
understanding of the world around us.

Asking questions is a crucial aspect of human
development and should be embraced for several reasons.
Firstly, asking questions helps us to learn and gain new
knowledge, enabling us to expand our minds and
understand new concepts. Secondly, asking questions
clarifies any confusion we may have or challenges any
misconceptions, leading to a clearer picture of the topic at
hand. Additionally, asking questions helps to challenge
assumptions and biases that we carry, broadening our
perspectives and stimulating critical thinking skills, which
are essential for problem-solving.

Furthermore, asking questions fosters curiosity, improves
communication and builds relationships with others. It
shows that we are interested in what they have to say,
leading to deeper conversations and a better understanding
of each other. Asking questions is also essential for
making better decisions. By gathering more information,

we can weigh up our options and consider all the relevant factors, leading to better-informed decisions.

Innovation is another benefit of asking questions. It can spark new ideas and lead to creative solutions to problems. In a constantly changing world, asking questions is crucial for adaptation to new situations and learning new skills.

Finally, asking questions helps us to grow and develop as individuals, challenging us to become better versions of ourselves.

Asking questions is an essential part of human development that should be embraced. It allows us to learn, grow and connect with others, leading to a better understanding of the world around us. Therefore, we should not be afraid to ask questions and should embrace our curiosity.

Asking questions is how we naturally learn

From the earliest stages of human development, it is evident that individuals are instinctively driven to learn and grow by asking questions. As a child, you likely demonstrated an insatiable curiosity by asking your parents and teachers countless questions in order to comprehend the world around you. As you progressed through life, you may have discovered that asking questions was an essential aspect of personal growth and development.

Despite this, you may have encountered instances where you felt hesitant or embarrassed to ask questions due to societal perceptions that view inquiry as a weakness or ignorance. However, asking questions is a powerful tool that facilitates personal growth and development. By embracing your innate curiosity and boldly seeking answers to your most pressing questions, you can broaden your knowledge, deepen your understanding of the world and develop new skills and abilities.

Thus, it is important not to be afraid to ask questions - no matter how insignificant or intricate they may appear. It is essential to recognise that seeking assistance is a sign of strength, not weakness. Approaching each situation with an open and curious mind unlocks a world of new possibilities and experiences.

The phrase "curiouser and curiouser" is from chapter two in Lewis Carroll's famous book *Alice's Adventures in Wonderland* (1865). It's said by Alice when she's exploring her new Wonderland and as she encounters various strange situations and characters. The line is often used to express a sense of wonder or confusion and, for Alice, it's in amazement at the peculiarities of the world she finds herself in. Specifically, she utters it when she grows in size after drinking from a bottle labelled 'Drink Me' and finds herself in a hall that is to too small for her.

The exact passage in the book goes as follows:

> *Alice opened the door and found that it led into a small passage, not much larger than a rat-*

hole: she knelt down and looked along the passage into the loveliest garden you ever saw. How she longed to get out of that dark hall, and wander about among those beds of bright flowers and those cool fountains, but she could not even get her head through the doorway; 'and even if my head would go through,' thought poor Alice, 'it would be of very little use without my shoulders. Oh, how I wish I could shut up like a telescope! I think I could, if I only know how to begin.' For, you see, so many out-of-the-way things had happened lately, that Alice had begun to think that very few things indeed were really impossible.

There seemed to be no use in waiting by the little door, so she went back to the table, half hoping she might find another key on it, or at any rate a book of rules for shutting people up like telescopes: this time she found a little bottle on it, ('which certainly was not here before,' said Alice,) and round the neck of the bottle was a paper label, with the words 'DRINK ME' beautifully printed on it in large letters.

It was all very well to say 'Drink me,' but the wise little Alice was not going to do that in a hurry. 'No, I'll look first,' she said, 'and see whether it's marked 'poison' or not'; for she had read several nice little histories about children who had got burnt, and eaten up by wild beasts and other unpleasant things, all because they would not remember the simple rules

their friends had taught them: such as, that a red-hot poker will burn you if you hold it too long; and

*that if you cut your finger very deeply with a knife,
it usually bleeds; and she had never forgotten that,
if you drink much from a bottle marked 'poison', it
is almost certain to disagree with you, sooner or
later.*

*However, this bottle was not marked
'poison', so Alice ventured to taste it, and finding it
very nice, (it had, in fact, a sort of mixed flavour of
cherry-tart, custard, pineapple, roast turkey, toffee,
and hot buttered toast,) she very soon finished it off.*

*'What a curious feeling!' said Alice; 'I must
be shutting up like a telescope'.*

*And so, it was indeed: she was now only ten
inches high, and her face brightened up at the
thought that she was now the right size for going
through the little door into that lovely garden. First,
however, she waited for a few minutes to see if she
was going to shrink any further: she felt a little
nervous about this; 'for it might end, you know,'
said Alice to herself, 'in my going out altogether,
like a candle. I wonder what I should be like then?'
And she tried to fancy what the flame of a candle is
like after the candle is blown out, for she could not
remember ever having seen such a thing.*

I wanted to explore the idea of asking questions or at least
look at the notion of how important it is to be curious
about what surrounds us. As Alice demonstrates, these
skills are also applicable to, albeit fictional, non-sales
situations. In doing so, I've added six more areas around
questioning in your personal life and about your personal
development in this second half of the book. However, in
the meantime, the following vignette was in the business

section in the last book, so I've move it here to kick off the second half of the book. I thought I'd start with an everyday situation many of us may find ourselves in and to be fair, I haven't done it myself for a while, so bear with.

Dating, you know, that process when you meet someone online, or your eyes meet across the frozen food aisle in the supermarket, or God forbid even old school, you ask someone you like at work to go for a drink.

I appreciate for many of us who are 'available' or 'on the market', the easy bit is done online now, i.e., swipe to the left or swipe to the right, it's a bit of a numbers game, but eventually you'll get a date in the diary.

Sales too is a numbers game, and a sales manager will assume that you'll close 25% of what's in your pipeline. However, you still need to keep it topped up with new prospects as it empties quickly with both wins and losses. I'm not suggesting of course that you apply this process to your dating efforts!

Anyway, back to the actual date. Assuming you've got lucky, on the special night, you might put on your favourite tunes whilst you have a long soak in the bath or get a hot shower, both options giving you time to imagine what your date is like in real life.

You put on a nice fragrance, not the one your younger brother bought you at Christmas, spend hours looking in the washing basket for something to wear, but chose your Sunday best/lucky knickers. You've arranged to meet in a trendy bar, you arrive, order sophisticated drinks like cocktails, not the normal pint or large house white, and the opening line you start with is,

'THIS IS A NICE PLACE, HAVE YOU BEEN HERE BEFORE?'

Good start, it's logical, it's not very controversial, you're showing some interest in your date, and you ask it with a smile but, chances are the answer is going to be a

'YES' OR 'NO'.

If it's a yes, you might possibly come back with,

'AHH, WAS THAT ON ANOTHER BLIND DATE??'

If that's also another

'YES',

you're getting squeezed into a corner now, so you

might then come back with, (if you can be any more stupid)

'BRILL, JUST RECENTLY?'

So, you can see where I'm going with this, exactly like the conversation on the date, nowhere.
What happens now, do you just stand there and stare at

each other?

Hopefully no. Rewind back to the start of the date and you'll begin by asking each other 'open ended' questions instead of the 'closed' questions above, with any luck your opening line will be more searching than a question like,

> *'ARE YOU ENJOYING THE NICE WEATHER
> AT THE MOMENT?'*

But instead, it might be more like,

> *'WHAT A LOVELY DAY, WHAT IS YOUR
> FAVOURITE MEMORY OF SUNNY DAYS WHEN
> YOU WERE A KID?'*

Yes, a bit cheesy, but done for dramatic effect! We'll come back to open and closed questions shortly as they're really important, not just to establish information in sales, but in everyday life as above. As mentioned earlier, following a little bit of research I did on the subject, I'm going to take a slight detour into the history and the importance of asking questions.

In a research document everything, and I mean everything, has to be referenced and cross referenced. In my own thesis document, I use the Harvard method of referencing to log every document, book, film, web page and radio broadcast, etc. that I've accessed and referred to in my work. That resulted in thirteen A4 pages. I'm not going to burden you much with this, it's not necessary, and it's probably not that important to you in the context of this book and, of course, we all know how to use Mr Google. If there's anything you want to know more about or follow up on that I discuss, Mr G. will be able to help you. More importantly, as well as giving you every question to ask in every sales situation, a breakdown of each stage of the sales process, the technical aspect and explaining the importance of good questioning techniques, I'm a writer, so I also want to tell you a story too.

Socratic questions

Let's take a journey back in time to ancient Greece where we can learn from the great philosopher Socrates. Despite living over 2,000 years ago, his teaching methods and philosophies are still relevant today.

Socrates was an early educator who believed in teaching by asking questions. His approach was focused on drawing out answers from his pupils through the disciplined practice of thoughtful questioning. By examining ideas and determining their validity, students could acknowledge contradictions, recreate inaccurate or unfinished ideas and critically evaluate their thoughts. He thought that:

> *'THE DISCIPLINED PRACTICE OF THOUGHTFUL QUESTIONING ENABLES THE SCHOLAR/STUDENT TO EXAMINE IDEAS AND BE ABLE TO DETERMINE THE VALIDITY OF THOSE IDEAS.*

Essentially, the teacher assumes an ignorant or naive mindset to compel the student to assume the highest level of knowledge.

Although Socrates was accused of corrupting the youth of Athens and was sentenced to death, he refused to escape punishment. He believed in his 'social contract' with the state and saw it as dishonourable to spurn the state. Despite this, he lived a frugal life and was known for his eccentricity.
Socrates' last words to Crito, his friend and believer in his ethical teachings were:

"CRITO, WE OWE A COCK TO ASCLEPIUS.
PLEASE, DON'T FORGET TO PAY THE DEBT

The quote in this next graphic is a powerful reminder that

"The only true wisdom is in knowing you know nothing."
Socrates

we should always approach new situations with an open mind and be willing to learn and question what we think we know.

Socrates' squestions

Following next are the six types of questions that Socrates would ask his pupils. Probably often to their initial annoyance but more often to their ultimate delight. He was a man of remarkable integrity and his story makes for enlightened reading if you find the time. There are many books available about the ancient Greek philosophers and their impact on our world today. I'm not allowed to put hyperlinks in this book, but Mr G. will be invaluable should you need him.

The overall purpose of Socratic questioning, is to challenge accuracy and completeness of thinking in a way that acts to move people towards their ultimate goal.

Conceptual clarification questions

Socrates wanted to get them to think more about what exactly they are asking or thinking about. Prove the concepts behind their argument and use basic 'tell me more' questions that get them to go deeper.

- Why are you saying that?
- What exactly does this mean?
- How does this relate to what we have been talking about?

- What is the nature of ...?
- What do we already know about this?
- Can you give me an example?
- Are you saying ... or ...?
- Can you rephrase that, please?

Probing assumptions

As Socrates probed their assumptions, it made them think about the presuppositions and unquestioned beliefs on which they are founding their argument. This was shaking the educational bedrock and got them really going!

- What else could we assume?
- You seem to be assuming ...?
- How did you choose those assumptions?
- Please explain why/how ...?
- How can you verify or disprove that assumption?
- What would happen if ...?
- Do you agree or disagree with ...?

Probing rationale, reasons, and evidence

Ultimately, they would have to give a rationale for their arguments, but Socrates would dig into that reasoning even more rather than assuming it is as a given.

- Why is that happening?
- How do you know this?
- Show me ...?
- Can you give me an example of that?
- What do you think causes...?
- What is the nature of this?
- Are these reasons good enough?
- Would it stand up in court?

How might it be refuted?

- How can I be sure of what you are saying?
- Why is ... happening?
- Why? (Keep asking it)
- What evidence is there to support it?
- On what authority are you basing your argument?

Questioning viewpoints and perspectives

Socrates argued that; most arguments are given from a particular position, so to challenge the assumption the student must attack that position and show that there are other, equally valid, viewpoints.

- Another way of looking at this is ..., does this seem reasonable?
- What alternative ways of looking at this are there?
- Why it is ... necessary?
- Who benefits from this?
- What is the difference between... and...?
- Why is it better than ...?
- What are the strengths and weaknesses of...?
- How are ... and ... similar?
- What would ... say about it?
- What if you compared ... and ...?
- How could you look another way at this?

Probe implications and consequences

He also suggested that the argument that they might give may have logical implications that can be forecast.

- Do these make sense?
- Are they desirable?
- Then what would happen?
- What are the consequences of that assumption?
- How could ... be used to ...?
- What are the implications of ...?
- How does ... affect ...?
- How does ... fit with what we learned before?
- Why is ... important?
- What is the best ...? Why?

Questions about the question

And finally, Socrates put forward the notion that it's possible to get reflexive about the whole thing, turning the question in on itself, using their argument or attack against themselves.

Put the ball back into their court.

- What was the point of asking that question?
- Why do you think I asked this question?
- Am I making sense? Why not?
- What else might I ask?
- What does that mean?

As you can see, Socratic questioning is a form of disciplined questioning that can be used to pursue thought in many directions and for many purposes, including: to explore complex ideas, to get to the truth of things, to open up issues and problems, to uncover assumptions, to analyse concepts, to distinguish what we know from what we do not know, to follow out logical consequences of thought or to control discussions.

Socratic questioning is based on the foundation that thinking has structured logic, and allows underlying thoughts to be questioned. The key to distinguishing Socratic questioning from questioning per se is that Socratic questioning is systematic, disciplined, deep and usually focuses on fundamental concepts, principles, theories, issues or problems.

Socratic questioning is referred to and used in modern teaching, and has gained a foothold as a concept in education, particularly in the past two decades. Teachers, students, or anyone interested in probing thinking at a deep level can construct Socratic questions and engage in these questions.

Socratic questioning and its variants have also been extensively used in psychotherapy.

Interestingly, nearly 2000 years later and 6000 miles west, Sir Joshua Girling Fitch's book 'The Art of Questioning,' was printed in 1879 and became a valuable manual for public school teachers. Not only does Girling Finch focus on the early questioning skills of Socrates, he argues that it is the definitive works on the subject.

While 'The Art of Questioning' may be a slim volume of 77 pages and barely 8,000 words, it is a valuable reading asset for teachers. This book provides an in-depth look at the importance of questioning and how to utilise it in teaching practices, a topic which is further explored in *The Awesome Power of Questions*, written by yours truly.

Fast forward another 110 years and the *Book of Questions* was written and published by Gregory Stock Ph.D. with an update and rewrite in 2013. This literarily is a book of questions to ask yourself or your friends and is fascinating. The first book, printed in 1987 unbelievably sold 2.5 million copies and was translated into 18 languages.

I've taken the liberty to reproduce Stocks first five questions and posted them next.

*TECHNOLOGY HAS BECOME A PART OF US.
WOULD YOU RATHER LOSE THE USE OF
ALL MOTORISED VEHICLES, ALL
TELECOMMUNICATION DEVICES AND
COMPUTERS OR ONE OF YOUR HANDS?*

*WHAT WOULD YOU DO IF YOUR 6-YEAR-
OLD DAUGHTER'S FAVOURITE TOY, A
TALKING DOLL, STARTED TRYING TO
CONVINCE HER THAT SHE NEEDED A NEW
FRIEND—THE NEXT DOLL IN THE
COMPANY'S LINE?*

*IF YOU HAD TO BE OBSESSED WITH
MONEY, SEX, SPORTS, RELIGION OR FOOD,
WHICH ONE WOULD YOU CHOOSE?*

*IGNORING ALL FINANCIAL
CONSIDERATIONS, WOULD YOU RATHER
SPEND THE NEXT 5 YEARS CONFINED TO*

AN URBAN MECCA LIKE NEW YORK CITY
OR A BEAUTIFUL, ISOLATED TOWN ON
THE CALIFORNIA COAST?

WOULD YOU RATHER WATCH AN
OLYMPICS THAT OUTLAWED
PERFORMANCE-ENHANCING DRUGS OR
ONE THAT EMBRACED THEM AND LET
ATHLETES USE MEDICAL PIT CREWS TO
JACK UP THEIR PERFORMANCES?

These are very thought-provoking I'm sure you'll
agree. More recently, Stock has just published something
similar for kids, again with some thought-provoking ideas.

Open and closed questions

Anyway, let's get back to the date in the trendy wine bar,
or in fact it could be any other normal or informal social
interaction. Open and closed questions are two types of
questions you have in your kit bag; however, they are very
different in character and usage. Asking the right
questions might not help you win the heart of your date,
but it will make them think you're interested in them and
not just in yourself.

For the sales people still with us at this point, you already
know that building rapport at the beginning is critical,
which of course is what you're trying to do
here on the first date in the wine bar.

C l o s e d   q u e s t i o n s

Definition

So, to give you something else to think about in the shower when you're getting ready for your date, there are two definitions that are used to describe closed questions.

The common definition is:

> *'A CLOSED QUESTION CAN BE ANSWERED WITH EITHER A SINGLE WORD OR A SHORT PHRASE'.*

For example, 'How old are you?' and 'Where do you live?' are closed questions, and to be fair are probably not the questions you want to start the date off with as you sip your 'Slippery Nipples' through a straw. A more limiting definition that is sometimes used is:

> *'A CLOSED QUESTION CAN BE ANSWERED WITH EITHER 'YES' OR 'NO'.*

Consequently, by using his definition 'Are you happy?' and 'Is that your final answer?' are closed questions, whilst 'What time is it?' and 'How old are you?' are not. This causes a problem of how to classify the short-answer non-yes-or-no questions,
which do not fit well with the definition for open questions. A way of handling this is to define 'yes-no' as a

sub-class of the short-answer closed question.

This might be too deep for thinking in the shower, but the point is, closed questions do have a role to play, perhaps a little later on in the date when you need to establish some finer detail, and once you have got to know each other a little better.

Using closed questions

Closed questions have the following characteristics:

- They give you facts
- They are easy to answer
- They are quick to answer
- They keep control of the conversation with the questioner

Closed-ended questions can be answered in only one word or with a short, specific piece of information. Closed-ended questions have the potential to end the conversation.

Here are examples of closed-ended questions in these types of situations:

- 'Would you like vanilla ice cream?'
- 'Have you ever met Joe before?'
- 'Where did you go to college?

- 'What is your best quality?'
- 'Are you happy?'
- 'Do you enjoy your car?'
- 'Does your brother have the same interests as you?'
- 'Do you have a pet?''
- 'Do you like animals?
- 'When is your birthday?'
- 'Do you like rain?

Note how you can turn any opinion into a closed question that forces a yes or no by adding tag questions, such as 'isn't it?', 'don't you?' or 'can't they?', to any statement. Tag questions are small questions added to the end of a statement, for example back to your date and the drinks:

'THAT LOOKS REFRESHING, IT'S A SLIPPERY NIPPLE, ISN'T IT?'

Note how the tag question turns the statement into a question.

Here are other tag type questions you can use:

- ..., won't you?
- ..., can't you?
- ..., shouldn't you?
- ..., don't they?
- ..., isn't it?
- ..., won't it?

Note the structural elements: The first element contains a verb, often 'to be' or 'to do', and is often a repetition of the verb used in the statement. The verb is negated and in the abbreviated form, the second element is a pronoun.

Using tag questions

By using a tag question to emphasise and encourage the other person to agree, they turn a bold assertion or command into a question that is difficult to disagree with.

Gaining Agreement

Make an assertion and add a tag question (Obviously in your own style)

> *'YOU'RE ENJOYING THE AVOCADO ON TOAST, AREN'T YOU?' (IT'S A TRENDY WINE BAR REMEMBER!)*

> *'YOU WILL HAVE THE SHARING PLATTER WITH ME, WON'T YOU?'*

Gaining Compliance

Clearly this is similar to getting agreement, so starting with what you want the other person to do, and then end with a tag such as 'won't you' or 'can't you'

> *YOU WILL COME TO THE NIGHTCLUB LATER, WON'T YOU?'.*

The first word of a question sets up the dynamic of the closed question and signals the easy answer ahead. Note how these are words like: do, would, are, will, if.

Open Questions

Definition

An open question can be described as:

'A QUESTION THAT IS LIKELY TO RECEIVE A LONG ANSWER'

Although any question can receive a long answer, open questions deliberately seek longer answers, and are the opposite of closed questions. Not only will they make the date or most social interactions more enjoyable and positive for both of you, you'll find out more about each other a lot quicker.

Using open questions

Open questions have the following characteristics:

- They ask the respondent to think and reflect.
- They will give you opinions and feelings.

- They hand control of the conversation to the respondent.

Open questions begin with such as: what, why, how, describe.

Using open questions can be scary, as they seem to hand control over to the other person. However, well-placed questions do leave you in control as you steer their interest and engage them where you want them. When opening conversations, a good balance is around three closed questions to one open question.

The closed questions start the conversation and summarise progress, whilst the open question gets the other person thinking and continuing to give you useful information about them.

A clever trick is to get them to ask you open questions. This then gives you the floor to talk about what you want. The way to achieve this is to intrigue them with an incomplete story or benefit.

I keep six honest
serving men

I suspect a book on questions isn't complete without a name check for Rudyard Kipling. No, not the guy who makes exceeding good pastries, but the author who gave us; *The Jungle Book, Gunga Din and The*

Man Who Would Be King.

Kipling was a journalist as well as a writer, so he understood the accuracy needed to ask the right questions to get to the real story. Whether the following poem (the first verse anyway) is inspired by requirements of his job I don't know, but he outlines a powerful set of questions. Again, I suspect but don't know, that he used these probing words in his interviews.

On the fun side, I like the idea of linking these two facts about him, without referencing as discussed earlier, but as this isn't an academic book, I can do that without getting into trouble with my director of studies. Happy days!

Whenever in doubt as to what to ask, just dip into this verse.

> I KEEP six honest serving-men
> (They taught me all I knew);
> Their names are What and Why and When
> And How and Where and Who.
> Rudyard Kipling – 1902

Cambridge.org suggested as its origin, a medieval Latin epigram in the Register of Daniel Rough, Clerk of Romney (and Fish Monger- Kent) in the 14th century, which reads:

> *SI SAPIENS FORE VIS SEX SERVUS*
> *QUI TIBI MANDO*

QUID DICAS ET UBI, DE QUO, CUR,
QUOMODO,

QUANDO.

(IF YOU WISH TO BE WISE, I COMMEND TO
YOU SIX SERVANTS,
ASK WHAT, WHERE, ABOUT WHAT, WHY,
HOW, WHEN.)

The most fascinating thing about research, even for a slim
and perceived modern subject book like this, is when you
do dig in you can uncover hidden treasures
and, in this case, the fact that everyone potentially does
have the odd skeleton in the cupboard, even Kipling.

Did he really steal it do you think, or does it just prove
that original thought is thin on the ground?

W h a t ?

'What?' often asks for noun responses, seeking things that
are or will be. 'What' questions might include:

- 'What are you doing?'
- 'What shall we do next?'
- 'What happened?'
- 'What is stopping you from succeeding?'
- 'What is the most important thing to do now?'
- Three 'What's' for example that might be asked in
  sequence to solve problems are:
- 'What are you trying to achieve?'

- 'What is the real problem?'
- 'What is the solution?'

W h y ?

Asking 'why' seeks cause-and-effect [1]. If you know the reason why people have done something, then you gain a deeper understanding of them. If you know how the world works, then you may be able to affect how it changes in the future.

Asking 'why' seeks logical connections and shows you to be rational in your thinking. It can also be a good way of creating a pause or distraction in a conversation, as many people make assertive statements but without knowing the real 'why' behind those assertions.

A reversal of 'Why' is to ask 'Why not', which is a wonderful creative challenge for stimulating people to think 'outside the box'. 'Why' questions include:

- 'Why did you do that?'
- 'Why did that happen?'
- 'Why is it important for us to try it again?'
- 'Why not give it a try?'

W h e n ?

'When' seeks location in time and can imply two different types of time. 'When', first of all, can ask for a specific single time, for example when a person will arrive at a given place or when an action will be completed. 'When' may also seek a duration, a period of time, such as when a person will take a holiday.

- 'When will you be finished?'
- 'When will you give me the money?'
- 'When are you taking your next holiday?'

H o w ?

'How' seeks verbs of process. They are hence good for probing into deeper detail of what has happened or what will happen.

- 'How did you achieve that?'
- 'How shall we get there?'
- 'How will you know she likes you?'
- 'How' can also be used with other words to probe into time and quantity.
- 'How often will you see me?'
- 'How much do you owe him?'

This can be quite effective for diverting attention away from the real question. For example, in the question above, the attention is on 'how often' and 'Seeing me' is assumed.

W h e r e ?

'Where' seeks to locate an action or event in three-dimensional space. This can be simple space, such as on, above, under, below. It can be regional space, such as next door or in the other building. It can be geographic space, such as New York, London or Paris.

If something is going to be delivered or done, then asking 'Where' is a very good companion to asking 'When', in order to clarify exactly what delivery will take place.

- 'Where will you put it?'
- 'Where will they be delivered?'
- Who will deliver it?

The question 'Who' brings people into the frame, connecting them with actions and things. The 'Who' of many situations includes 'stakeholders', who are all the people with an interest in the action. Key people to identify are those who will pay for and receive the benefits of the action. Of course, you also may want to know who is going to do the work and whose neck is on the line -- that is who is ultimately responsible.

- 'Who is this work for?'
- 'Who will benefit most from what you propose?'
- 'Who else would be interested?'

Assumptive Questions

Kipling questions provide a simple method of using assumptive questions that act as if something is true, then hide it in a question:

- 'How much do you care?' (Assumption: you care)

- 'How will you persuade her'? (Assumption: you will seek to persuade her)
- 'Where will you buy it?' (Assumption: you will buy it)
- 'When will you make the change?' (Assumption: you will make the change)
- Solving Problems

A simple framework for solving problems may be defined by combining What, Why and How, as follows:

- 'What is the problem?'
- 'Why is it happening?'
- 'How can you fix it'
- '– Fix it! – '
- 'Why did it work or not work?'
- 'What next?'

I'm sure I've resolved absolutely none of your dating problems, but it was a bit of fun to go off piste slightly for a few paragraphs. But time is money so we need to free-ride back to the groomed slopes and to the reason you bought this book, hopefully which was to understand how to ask the right questions at the right time, and in the right situation.

Well, if you haven't already, find yourself somewhere a quite spot, get a pen and a coffee, and highlight the questions that you're going to start to include in your sales calls, or your next date.

Does life get in your way?

Asking questions is one of the most powerful tools for personal growth, communication, problem-solving, building relationships and learning. It allows us to deepen our understanding of ourselves and others, improve our decision-making skills and expand our knowledge and perspectives. In this modern age of information overload, the ability to ask the right questions has become increasingly valuable.

Whether we're seeking personal growth, professional development, or simply trying to navigate the complexities of daily life, asking questions is a crucial skill that can help us achieve our goals and live more fulfilling lives. In this section, we will explore the various benefits of asking questions and how it can enhance different areas of our lives.

Why asking questions is important in relationships:

- Building trust: Asking questions and actively listening to the responses can help build trust in the relationship.
- Improving communication: Asking questions can clarify misunderstandings, ensure both parties are on the same page, and facilitate more meaningful conversations.
- Strengthening connections: By showing a genuine interest in the other person's life and experiences, we can deepen our relationships.
- Resolving conflicts: Asking questions can help us understand the other person's perspective and work towards a resolution that works for both parties.
- Learning and growing together: By sharing our own experiences and asking questions, we can learn from each other and grow together.
- Why asking questions is important in communication.
- Encouraging active listening: Asking questions shows that you are interested in what the other person has to say, encouraging them to speak openly and honestly.
- Promoting empathy: Asking questions helps you to understand the other person's perspective and feelings, increasing your empathy and compassion.

- Avoiding assumptions: Asking questions helps you avoid making assumptions about the other person's thoughts, feelings, and intentions.
- Clarifying misunderstandings: Asking questions can clarify any misunderstandings or miscommunications that may have occurred.
- Building trust: Asking questions and listening actively shows the other person that you value and respect them, building trust and strengthening the relationship.
- Why asking questions is important for self-awareness:
- Deepening understanding of ourselves: Asking introspective questions can help identify our values, beliefs, motivations and areas for improvement.
- Seeking feedback: Asking for feedback from others can provide valuable insights into our strengths and weaknesses.
- Communicating effectively: Being self-aware allows us to communicate more effectively with others.
- Why asking questions is important for problem-solving:
- Encouraging creativity: Asking open-ended questions can help explore different possibilities and generate creative solutions.
- Fostering collaboration: Problem-solving questions can involve others in finding solutions, fostering collaboration and teamwork.
- Improving decision-making: Asking targeted questions can help identify the root cause of a

problem and make informed decisions based on available information.

- Increasing self-awareness: Asking questions about our own thought process and decision-making can improve self-awareness.
- Boosting confidence: Successfully solving problems through effective questioning can boost confidence and improve problem-solving skills over time.
- Why asking questions is important for learning.
- Acquiring new knowledge: Asking questions allows us to explore new concepts and ideas and gain a deeper understanding of the world around us.
- Refining and expanding knowledge: Asking questions helps us refine and expand our existing knowledge and consider multiple perspectives.
- Identifying gaps in knowledge: Asking questions can help identify gaps in our knowledge and seek out answers to fill those gaps, leading to more comprehensive understanding.

Questions let you reflect

Self-reflection is not just a one-time event; it should be a regular practice that you make a habit of. It is essential to set aside dedicated time for reflection, as it helps you gain clarity, identify your strengths and weaknesses and make progress towards your goals. In this fast-paced world, we often get caught up in the hustle and bustle of life, and we forget to take a step back and reflect on our lives. However, making self-reflection a habit can lead to a more fulfilling life.

Successful people across various industries often credit regular self-reflection for their success. By taking the time to reflect on their past experiences and decisions, they can learn from their mistakes, identify what works for them and make better choices in the future. By making self-reflection a regular practice, you can also gain insights into your life and make better decisions that align with your values and goals.

To make self-reflection a habit, it is essential to set aside dedicated time each week for reflection. This could be as little as ten minutes a day or an hour a week. Some people prefer to keep a journal to track their progress, while others prefer self-reflection is an essential tool for personal growth and development. By taking the time to look inward, we can gain insights into our own behaviours, thought patterns and emotions.
Asking ourselves thoughtful questions is a key part of this

process and here are some examples of questions that can help guide your self-reflection:

- How did I feel during the time of 'the' incident?
- Did I experience any particular emotions, such as anger, frustration or sadness?
- How did those emotions affect my behaviour or my relationships with others?
- Is there anything that bothered me over the week that I haven't addressed?
- What has been weighing on my mind lately, and why?
- Is there something I need to confront or resolve in order to move forward?
- How did I react when 'that' event happened?
- Was my response reflexive or deliberate?
- What triggered my reaction, and was it in line with my values or goals?
- How can I communicate my needs and boundaries more effectively in the future?
- Am I clear about my own wants and needs, and am I expressing them assertively yet respectfully?
- Do I feel fulfilled in my work or other aspects of my life?
- If not, what is missing or unsatisfying, and how can I address that?
- What can I do to improve my situation?
- What specific steps can I take to change my circumstances or my outlook on them?
- What is the takeaway from 'the' mistake I made?

- What can I learn from this experience, and how can I use that knowledge to avoid similar errors in the future?
- How can I better align my actions with my values or goals?
  - Am I living in a way that is consistent with my beliefs and aspirations?
  - What would be a wiser way to handle things if this issue arises again?
  - What alternative approaches or perspectives could I consider, and how might they lead to a better outcome?

We are all busy people, often with lots of plates spinning. However, it's important to do a 'stock check' of our lives every now and then, even if it's just to confirm to ourselves we are on the right path and doing everything we can to live our lives the best we can. Consequently, I've gathered some further self-reflective prompts that can encourage you to even deeper thinking or exploration:

- What are your core values?
- How do these values influence your daily decisions and actions?
- Are there any instances where your actions do not align with your values? If so, how can you address this?
- What are your strengths and weaknesses?
- How can you leverage your strengths to overcome your weaknesses?
- Are there any skills or knowledge areas you would like to develop further?

- How can you incorporate this into your personal or professional growth plan?
- What motivates you?
- What are your passions? How can you incorporate these into your daily life or career?
- Are there any obstacles that are preventing you from pursuing your passions?
- How can you overcome them?
- What have been some significant challenges or failures in your life?
- How have these experiences shaped you as a person?
- How can you use these experiences as a learning opportunity and grow from them?
- Are there any patterns or habits that you can change to prevent similar challenges or failures in the future?
- What are your long-term goals?
- How do your current actions align with these goals?
- Are there any adjustments you need to make to your daily routine or habits to achieve these goals?
- How can you hold yourself accountable to stay on track?

These prompts can encourage deeper thinking and exploration into your values, passions and goals. You can use them as a starting point for self-reflection and connect your answers to broader themes or values that are important to you. Remember, self-reflection is an ongoing process, and it's essential to make it a habit to continue growing and learning as a person.

Remember, self-reflection is an ongoing process, not a one-time event. By asking ourselves these and other probing questions, we can gain deeper insights into ourselves and our place in the world. Make reflection a regular habit, and don't be afraid to dive deep into the answers. The more honest and introspective you can be, the more you'll grow and evolve over time.

Questions help you find answers

Asking the right questions can also help you reframe your challenges in a more positive light, leading to new perspectives and potential solutions. It can help you identify the underlying assumptions or beliefs

that are holding you back, and challenge them in a constructive way. This process of questioning can also help you develop a growth mindset, where challenges are viewed as opportunities for learning and growth, rather than roadblocks.

Additionally, asking questions can help you make more informed decisions by gathering relevant information and perspectives from others. This can lead to better outcomes and prevent potential pitfalls that may have been overlooked otherwise.

However, it's important to remember that asking questions is not just about finding answers, but also about building relationships and fostering open communication. By showing genuine curiosity and interest in others' perspectives, you can establish trust and create a more collaborative environment. This can lead to stronger connections with colleagues, friends, and family, as well as deeper understanding and empathy for others.

In short, asking questions is an essential tool for navigating the challenges of life, fostering personal growth and building stronger relationships. Don't be afraid to ask questions, even if they seem basic or trivial – the insights and perspectives you gain can be invaluable.

Asking questions benefits your mind

By asking questions and seeking answers, you can cultivate a deeper understanding of yourself and the world around you, nurturing your mind and enriching your life. Following are some really good benefits and positive internal improvements that can develop from asking good questions:

Improved Decision Making

Asking questions helps you gather more information, which can lead to better decision making. When you ask the right questions, you can gain insights that can help you choose the best path forward. By seeking input from others, you may also be exposed to new perspectives that can challenge your assumptions and broaden your thinking.

Increased Creativity

Asking questions can spark creativity and innovation by helping you think beyond the status quo. By questioning the way things are done or considering alternative approaches, you can generate new ideas and perspectives that can lead to breakthroughs and innovative solutions.

Improved Communication

Asking questions is also an important part of effective communication. By asking open-ended questions and actively listening to the answers, you can build stronger relationships with others and establish rapport. Asking questions can also help you clarify your own thoughts and ideas, making it easier to communicate them to others.

Self-Discovery

Asking questions of yourself can also help you better

understand your own thoughts, feelings and motivations. By exploring your own beliefs and assumptions, you can gain greater self-awareness and identify areas for personal growth and development.

Relationships

Asking questions can also help you build stronger relationships with others. By showing interest in their thoughts and feelings, you can deepen your connection and demonstrate empathy. Asking questions can also help you avoid misunderstandings and conflicts by clarifying expectations and assumptions

Wisdom

Questioning the things around you makes your brain more flexible, allowing for better perception, more tolerance and understanding, and an increased ability to be unbiased in your life.

Flexibility

When you ask questions, new signals and patterns in the brain are formed, pinging back and forth. The more patterns the brain creates in this process, the more likely it is to become flexible. In this context, being flexible means accessing additional stored memories and information without returning to a previous, less-functional state.

Positive Thinking

Asking questions, especially if it's difficult for you, gives you a better understanding of how much control you have over your life and actions. This can help you feel more at peace with yourself as you learn to regulate and manage your emotions for the future.

Asking questions give you better answers

When it comes to objective truths or facts, the answer is often clear-cut and straightforward. For example, if you want to know the capital city of a particular country, you can look it up and get a definitive answer. In such cases, relying solely on your own insight or knowledge might be sufficient.

However, many dilemmas are subjective in nature, meaning that there may be multiple valid perspectives or solutions to the problem. In these cases, seeking outside opinions and ideas can be incredibly helpful in gaining a broader understanding of the issue and exploring alternative solutions. By doing so, you can benefit from the experiences and insights of others, which can help you see the problem in a new light and come up with a more creative or effective solution.

Additionally, seeking input from others can help you identify blind spots or biases that might be affecting your thinking. By getting feedback and input from people with different perspectives or experiences, you can get a more complete picture of the problem and avoid making decisions based on incomplete or inaccurate information.

This is because:

- Getting outside opinions and perspectives can also challenge your assumptions and beliefs, helping you to see the situation from a different angle and consider new possibilities.
- Collaborating with others can also foster a sense of community and support, reducing feelings of isolation and overwhelm.
- Asking for help can also build trust and rapport with others, strengthening your relationships and social connections.
- Seeking input from others can also help you learn and grow, as you may encounter new ideas or approaches that you haven't considered before. This can lead to personal and professional development, and expand your knowledge and skillset.
- In some cases, seeking help or input from others can also lead to better decision-making, as you weigh the pros and cons of different options and consider the potential outcomes more thoroughly.

- More perspectives give you more ideas to tackle the situation – and more combined years of experience behind it all.
- Your brain automatically jumps to the first solution it thinks of and can benefit from other ideas.
- Other people offer unbiased answers to your situations; you may be too close to your own situation to find a truly rational answer on your own

Asking questions helps you learn and understand, (rather than judging or assuming)

It's easy for human beings to slip into the bad habit of judging others instead of seeking to learn their point of view. You can break this habit or pattern by learning to ask polite questions before you even think of judging someone.

This is clearly a positive trait, as it:

- Encourages empathy: When you ask polite questions instead of jumping to judgment, you open yourself up to the other person's perspective and experiences. This allows you to cultivate empathy and understanding towards others, rather than simply writing them off or dismissing them.

- Promotes open-mindedness: By asking questions and being open to learning about someone else's point of view, you become more open-minded and receptive to new ideas and perspectives.
- Builds stronger relationships: Asking polite questions shows that you are interested in the other person and value their input. This can lead to stronger and more positive relationships, as well as better communication and collaboration.
- Helps you learn and grow: By actively seeking out different perspectives and asking questions, you expose yourself to new ideas and experiences. This can help you learn and grow as a person, and expand your own worldview.
- Stops you from hurrying in.
- Gives you the chance to gather all needed information.
- Informs you whether a solution is needed.
- Keeps you trained on the big picture.

Here's a list of questions that aim to promote learning and understanding without judgment or assumptions:

- 'What would you like to share about your experience or perspective on this topic?'
- 'How would you describe your understanding of this concept or idea?'
- 'Can you provide more details or examples to help me better grasp your viewpoint?'
- 'What sources or references have influenced your thinking on this subject?'

- 'What do you believe are the key factors or considerations that contribute to this situation?'
- 'What are some potential alternative explanations or interpretations that we should explore?'
- 'Are there any specific terms or concepts that you feel are important to define or clarify?'
- 'How do you envision the ideal outcome or solution in this scenario?'
- 'Can you walk me through the steps or thought process that led you to this conclusion?'
- 'What additional information or data do you think would be valuable to consider in this context?'
- 'Have you encountered any counterarguments or opposing viewpoints that have influenced your thinking?'
- 'Can you help me understand the reasons behind your preference or choice in this matter?'
- 'Are there any underlying assumptions or biases that may be shaping your perspective?'
- 'How do you think this issue or idea relates to other related topics or fields?'
- 'What are the potential implications or consequences of different courses of action in this situation?'

These questions aim to foster an open and non-judgmental dialogue, allowing for a deeper understanding of someone's viewpoint or perspective.

Questions encourages cooperation

Asking questions is not only a good ice-breaker, but it also facilitates collaboration and can teach valuable lessons in teamwork and leadership. Working with others towards a common goal requires effective communication, and questioning is a vital part of that process. By asking questions, you can ensure that everyone is on the same page and that everyone's ideas are heard and considered.

Collaboration has been proven to be more effective than working alone, and asking questions is a key element of successful collaboration. It helps to break down barriers and encourages everyone to contribute their ideas and expertise. Additionally, asking questions demonstrates humility and a willingness to learn from others, which can foster a positive and productive team dynamic.

It's important to note that effective collaboration cannot be achieved if you act as if you are above everyone else. Asking questions shows that you value the input of others and are willing to listen to their ideas. This can inspire others to do the same, leading to better teamwork, idea-sharing and, ultimately, success.

Questions help you become a better leader

It's a common misconception that leaders should always have all the answers. However, the best leaders know the power of asking questions and actively seeking input from their team members.

In fact, studies have shown that leaders who ask more questions tend to be viewed as more effective. This is because asking questions demonstrates a willingness to learn, an openness to new ideas, and a genuine interest in the opinions and perspectives of others.

Furthermore, when you ask questions as a leader, you can gather valuable information that can help you make better decisions and solve problems more effectively. By involving your team members in the decision-making process, you not only show them that you value their input, but you also foster a sense of ownership and accountability among the group.

So don't be afraid to ask questions as a leader. By doing so, you can build stronger relationships with your team, gain valuable insights and ultimately become a more effective and respected leader.

People will like you more

Have you ever noticed that people tend to like you more when you show an interest in them? Asking questions is a great way to make a positive impression and build rapport with others.

Here are some reasons why asking questions can help you connect with others:

- Reciprocity: When you show an interest in others by asking questions, they are more likely to reciprocate by showing an interest in you.
- Self-disclosure: People enjoy talking about themselves, and asking questions can encourage them to open up and share more about themselves.
- Active listening: By actively listening and responding to what others are saying, you demonstrate that you are engaged and interested in the conversation.
- Memorable conversations: Asking unique or thought-provoking questions can leave a lasting impression and make the conversation more memorable.

So next time you're meeting someone new or catching up with an old friend, try asking questions and see how it helps you build a stronger connection.

When You Ask Questions, it can influence others

If you're looking to ask questions that might broaden someone's perspective or encourage critical thinking, here are a few examples:

- 'What evidence supports your opinion?'
- 'Can you explain your reasoning behind that idea?'
- 'Have you considered any alternative perspectives?'
- 'What assumptions are you making in this situation?'
- 'How do you think others might be affected by this decision?'
- 'What are the potential consequences of taking that action?'
- 'What are the underlying values driving your beliefs?'
- 'Can you help me understand how you arrived at that conclusion?'
- 'What if the situation were reversed? How would you feel then?'
- 'What other options do you see for addressing this problem?'

Remember, the goal of asking questions is not to manipulate someone, but to encourage critical thinking, broaden perspectives and promote open and honest dialogue.

Asking questions can also make other people feel important

If you encounter difficulty connecting with people and engaging with them on a deeper level, one of the best ways to draw someone out and get to know them

is by asking interesting questions. By asking the right questions, you can stimulate more exciting and fun conversations, set the stage for discovering common interests, developing a more authentic connection and fostering mutual empathy and understanding. Asking these questions to get to know people reveals something about yourself as well, showing others that you are engaged, interested and aware of their value as a person.

This invites authentic and genuine sharing and connection, setting a foundation for a lasting, mutually satisfying relationship.

There are many more I'm sure, but to give you a good start I've listed below some of the questions that I find interesting to ask when you're trying to get to know them, not in any particular order:

- 'What is your best childhood memory?'
- 'If you had a chance to do something differently in life, what would you change?'
- 'How did the two of you meet?'

- 'What do you feel most proud of?'
- 'What is your favourite music?'
- 'If you could travel anywhere, where would you go and why?'
- 'If you could only keep five possessions, what would they be?'
- 'What teacher in school made the most impact on you and why?'
- 'What do you want your tombstone to say?'
- 'What was one of your most defining moments in life?'
- 'Why did you choose your profession?'
- 'How do you spend your free time?'
- 'If you won the lottery, what would you do?'
- 'Who do you most admire in life?'
- 'What are your top three favourite books and why?'
- 'What are you most afraid of?'
- 'What feels like love to you?'
- 'If you could have any superpower, what would it be and why?'
- 'What is your favourite food?'
- 'What is your idea of a perfect day?'
- 'What motivates you?'
- 'What is your greatest accomplishment?'
- 'What is the most interesting place you have visited?'
- 'What do you think is the meaning of life?'
- 'What is your biggest goal in life?'
- 'What would you do if you only had one week to live?'
- 'What is your favourite quote and why?'

- 'What is your favourite season and why?'
- 'What do you think is the most important quality in a person?'

Critical Thinking

Critical thinking is important both professionally and personally, it can help your with:

- Better decision-making: Critical thinking helps in making informed decisions by analysing and evaluating information objectively. This skill is essential in the workplace and in personal life, where you are faced with a variety of decisions that require careful consideration.
- Problem-solving: Critical thinking skills help individuals identify problems and find practical solutions to them. This is an important skill for both personal and professional success.
- Improved communication: Critical thinking skills allow individuals to express their ideas and opinions more effectively and to communicate with others in a clear, concise and persuasive manner. This skill is particularly important in the workplace, where effective communication is essential for success.
- Adaptability: Critical thinking skills allow individuals to adapt to new situations and challenges quickly. This skill is important in the workplace, where employees are often required to adapt to changing circumstances and new technologies.
- Creativity: Critical thinking skills can stimulate creativity and innovation. By thinking critically, individuals can identify new and creative solutions to problems, which can lead to personal and professional success.

Overall, critical thinking skills are important for personal and professional growth, and can help individuals make better decisions, solve problems effectively, communicate more clearly and adapt to new situations.

Questions to encourage critical thinking

- 'What is the source of your information?'
- 'How would your perspective differ if you were on the opposing side?'
- 'How can we find a creative solution to this problem?'
- 'What is your position on this issue, and why do you agree or disagree?'
- 'Why is that your answer?'
- 'How can we prevent this problem from recurring in the future?'
- 'Why is this topic relevant today?'
- 'What is another perspective on this issue?'

- 'Can you provide an example?'
- 'How could the outcome have been different?'
- 'When can we determine if the solution is effective?'
- 'Why did you ask that question?'
- 'Who will be affected by this, and how?'

- 'What can we learn from this story, and how does it relate to our lives?'
- 'Why is this issue a problem, and how can we solve it?'

Questions help you to rethink a situation

Sometimes, asking questions can lead you to an answer that challenges your beliefs or expectations. This can be a jarring experience, but it's important to maintain a positive attitude. Rather than viewing this as a setback, try to see it as an opportunity for growth. When you are forced to reconsider your perspectives, you have the chance to expand your knowledge and learn something new.

Embrace the discomfort and use it as a catalyst for personal and intellectual growth. By staying open-minded and receptive to new ideas, you can become a more well-rounded and informed individual. Some situations to consider include:

- Relationships: By asking questions, we can better understand our partners, friends and family members. We can learn about their thoughts, feelings and experiences, which can help us connect with them on a deeper level.
- Communication: Asking questions can improve our communication skills, helping us to express

ourselves more clearly and to understand others better. By asking questions, we can avoid misunderstandings and ensure that our messages are getting across effectively.

- Self-awareness: Asking ourselves questions can help us become more self-aware. We can reflect on our thoughts, emotions and behaviours, and gain insight into our strengths and weaknesses.
- Problem-solving: When faced with a challenge, asking questions can help us identify the root cause of the problem and come up with effective solutions.
- Learning: Asking questions can help us learn new things and expand our knowledge. By asking questions, we can seek out information and gain a deeper understanding of the world around us.

Grow your knowledge and awareness (to boost your success)

Being able to ask the right questions in social situations can have a range of personal benefits. Firstly, it allows you to better understand and connect with the people you are interacting with. By asking open-ended questions, you demonstrate interest and engagement in their thoughts and feelings, which can help to build rapport and trust.

Asking the right questions can also help you to navigate tricky social situations with more ease. For example, if you are in a disagreement with someone, asking questions about their perspective can help you to better understand their point of view and find common ground. This can lead to more productive and positive outcomes in the long run.

Furthermore, asking the right questions can help you to develop your own critical thinking skills and broaden your knowledge base. By engaging in thoughtful and curious questioning, you challenge your assumptions and expand your understanding of the world. This can lead to personal growth and increased confidence in your own abilities to navigate social dynamics and complex situations.

Examining the biographies of accomplished individuals reveals intriguing trends, such as their capacity to inquire in a childlike manner. Distinguished achievers comprehend the limitations of their knowledge and expertise, a trait that sets them apart from the majority. Frequently, people tend to overestimate their comprehension of the world after achieving success in a particular field, and they are apprehensive about appearing foolish after attaining a prominent position in society.

Nevertheless, high-performing individuals exhibit humility and demonstrate their intellect by posing questions, not by flaunting their knowledge. This approach enables them to learn from others and cultivate trustworthy relationships. The sagacious recognise the value of introspection and reflect on their actions to evaluate their progress and ascertain whether they are headed in the right direction. By engaging in this behaviour, individuals can enhance their self-awareness and bolster their confidence. The insights that arise from the examination can aid in making astute decisions and navigating obstacles.

In essence, questioning oneself frequently is the optimal approach to remain focused and achieve one's full potential. With that in mind, let us examine some internal enquiries for self-awareness and use them to our advantage.

On Personality and Interests

- What makes you feel great?
- And what drains your energy?
- What are your strengths and superpowers?
- And what are your flaws and weaknesses?
- What do you get compliments about?
- What do you enjoy doing – even without rewards?
- How do you like to distract yourself and escape reality?

On Challenges and Personal Growth

- What did you learn recently?
- When do you feel most productive?
- What are your biggest challenges and fears?
- What's the smallest thing you could start doing to face your fears?

On Self-Image and Focus

- How would you describe yourself?
- What do you think about yourself?

- Do you focus on solutions or on reasons why you cannot?
- How would you rate your self-confidence and esteem?

On Emotional and Social Intelligence

- How would you describe yourself emotionally?
- How would you describe your communication style?
- What traits in others annoy you?
- What's the last time you complimented someone?

On Priorities and Habits

- What is most important to you?
- And do you focus your time on those important things?
- What are the good and bad habits you've developed?
- What is a single habit that would significantly improve your life?

On Impact and Personal Success

- If you could change one thing in the world, what would you change?
- What is your definition of success?
- What does your perfect day look like?
- How would you like people to remember you?

Answering these questions truthfully can provide valuable personal insights, allowing you to make decisions that align with your desires and navigate through challenging situations. Self-awareness is essential in creating a fulfilling life that matches your unique needs and aspirations.

Sometimes people believe that achieving their perfect life is unattainable, especially when significant changes are required. However, making a few bold changes can be enough to transform your life in a meaningful way.

Even if you are content with your current situation, answering these questions can help you confirm that you are on the right path. It is easy to get swept up in the day-to-day routine and neglect to take a step back to reflect on your progress and future goals. These self-awareness questions provide an opportunity to ensure that you are staying focused and headed towards your ideal life.

End Matter-Part Two

It's important to ask the right Questions, and this last list provides the overall benefits to you when you do. But, as I said earlier, it's vital to know how to use the answers and what they can do for you. In summary they can:

- Build rapport fosters stronger relationships with others.
- Nurture creativity by encouraging brainstorming and out-of-the-box thinking.
- Grow your knowledge and awareness by exposing you to different perspectives and information.
- Exercise critical thinking and problem-solving skills by challenging assumptions and exploring alternatives.
- Make the other person feel valued and heard, leading to more productive and positive interactions.
- Help you make thoughtful decisions by providing a deeper understanding of the situation and options available.
- The better our questions, the better our answers, leading to better outcomes and results.
- Keep you agile and open to new ideas and possibilities, allowing for growth and adaptability.
- Improve your memory and retention by engaging in active listening and processing of information.
- Help you stay informed and relevant by seeking out new knowledge and staying curious.

- Enable you to discover a new world of possibilities you would not have known otherwise, leading to personal and professional growth.

And finally ...

I've been studying 'Questions' for a long time. Over the last ten years, especially during my research, it's been in a more clinical environment. Whilst I'm delighted to discuss Socratic questioning in an educational or sales setting, questions also have a vital use in other areas, such as grief therapy.

In his paper *Creative Writers and Day-Dreaming* (1907), Sigmund Freud argued that keeping a journal or writing creatively, whilst not a 'cure' for grief, did facilitate healing. It wasn't until the 1980s, after the James Pennebaker's 'expressive writing' trials, that writing-as-therapy was considered a serious method of clinical practice (US).

In grief therapy, questions are often referred to as

Prompts, usually through a journal. They provide targeted questions that allow the sufferer to focus on aspects of their grief by writing their thoughts down. This draws out the main areas of pain, allowing them to confront it and ultimately come to terms with the death of their loved one.

While I've updated this book with the wellbeing and the softer aspects of using questions in the second half of the book, it did give me the idea to look at journaling. So, in the meantime I've also written four other books using journal prompts. They are designed like a journal but I've also written a background to grief plus an explanation of why self-expressive writing can help in grief recovery.

The first book is *Remember with Love* (2023). This is a self-help book for a parent or guardian to help support a child (between 4-10) after they've lost a pet. There is also a simply explanation of death and dying alongside 100 prompts.

The second book *Grief Tools* (2023), is for adults who have lost a child. This also draws on my own experience as well as my research. The third book is for adults who have lost a loved one, for example a partner, parent or a close friend. The fourth book, is for young adults (11-16) who have lost a pet. There's a least one more in the pipeline, all under the series 'Left Us too Soon'. These books are all on Amazon.

That is not a good SVP I know, and apologies for the

plug and sales pitch for my new books. Nonetheless, the subject of grief is really important to me, so thank you for your indulgence.

I hope all the information I've provided, especially this book, has been useful to you and I wish you every success in the future.

Good Luck!

About the Author

Ian is a business professional with an unexpected twist – he holds a Ph.D. in Creative Writing. His doctoral thesis focused into the therapeutic use of creative writing to cope with grief. A heavy subject not for the fainthearted.

Though it may not seem relevant to this book, there's a profound reason for it.

Tragedy struck when Ian's eldest son, Dom, lost his life in a car accident caused by a drunk driver on October 4th, 2013. This devastating event shook Ian to his core. Amidst the grief and despair, Ian found solace in writing. He believes that without his family and the power of writing, he might not have made it to the point where you now hold his book.

The death of a child before its parents is against the natural order of things. It leaves countless questions unanswered in a parent's mind. For Ian, writing provided an outlet to express and explore these overwhelming thoughts. Throughout his Ph.D. research, he documented his actions, experiences and the ruminations of a grieving father. The result was a poignant personal memoir titled *Grief and Other Minds*. 78,000 words of honesty and raw emotion.

While *The Awesome Power of Questions* focuses on the art of questioning, it's worth acknowledging that Ian's background in grief and grief recovery has influenced his work.

Having spent ten years in academia, Ian brings a wealth of knowledge to this book, his extensive research has contributed to its depth and authenticity.

www.ianploftus.com

Bibliography

Einstein (1959)

Euripides (407 B.C.)

Freud, S. (1907), *Creative Writers and Day-Dreaming*

Girling Finch, J., (1879). *The Art of Questions*. Bardeen. (Reprint 2010 Kessler Publishing)

Kipling. R., (1900). I keep six honest serving men. Ladies' Home Journal.

King, M L, (1963)

Lewis, C. (1865) *Alice's Adventures in Wonderland* Macmillan & Co., London, England

Plato (347 B.C.)

Socrates (399 B.C.)